PRAISE FOR

DATING SUCKS, BUT YOU DON'T

··

"*Dating Sucks, but You Don't* is smart, funny, classy, and practical as fuck. Connell's stories will make you laugh—and sometimes cringe—and his advice will transform your dating life without turning you into a douche. It's the book all single guys need to read now, and exactly what our culture needs at this moment."
—Mike Sacks, editor at *Vanity Fair*, *New York Times*
bestselling author of *Poking A Dead Frog*

"This is not just a book about how to attract the right woman. It's about how to be a better man."
—Sean Abrams, AskMen's sex and dating editor

"This book is a wake-up call for men to reject toxic masculinity and embrace empathy and vulnerability. It's a must-read for single men in the #MeToo era."
—Mike Johnson, *Bachelorette* star, Instagram influencer,
bestselling author of *Making the Love You Want*

"Dating in L.A. sucks. It's refreshing to read a book that teaches guys what women really want: true authenticity. There's nothing sexier than a man who knows who he is."
—Ione Butler, actress, bestselling author of *Uplifting Stories*

"To find the woman of your dreams, you need confidence, a positive mindset, and a tested, step-by-step plan. This book gives you all three."
—Jim Fannin, peak-performance coach for elite athletes
and businesses, bestselling author of *The Blueprint*

"This book helps good-hearted guys find love without having to use any 'pickup' tricks or play any games. Nice guys do finish first."
—Karen Salmansohn, bestselling author of books that have sold
more than two million copies, including *Happy Habits*

DATING SUCKS

SUCKS

But

YOU DON'T

CONNELL BARRETT

DATING SUCKS
But
YOU DON'T

THE

MODERN GUY'S
GUIDE TO

TOTAL CONFIDENCE,

ROMANTIC CONNECTION,

AND FINDING

THE PERFECT PARTNER

SIMON ELEMENT

New York   London   Toronto   Sydney   New Delhi

SIMON ELEMENT

An Imprint of Simon & Schuster, Inc.
1230 Avenue of the Americas
New York, NY 10020

First Simon Element trade paperback edition June 2022

SIMON ELEMENT and colophon are trademarks of Simon & Schuster, Inc.

For information about special discounts for bulk purchases, please contact Simon & Schuster Special Sales at 1-866-506-1949 or business@simonandschuster.com.

The Simon & Schuster Speakers Bureau can bring authors to your live event. For more information or to book an event, contact the Simon & Schuster Speakers Bureau at 1-866-248-3049 or visit our website at www.simonspeakers.com.

Interior design by Jennifer Chung

Stop icon by Adrien Coquet/The Noun Project
Sleep, Wink, In Love, and Happy icons by Jo Santos/The Noun Project
Cow icon by Rutmer Zijlstra/The Noun Project
Poop icon by Icon Island/The Noun Project
Deadpan icon by Gregory Mack/The Noun Project
Eggplant icon by AomAm/The Noun Project
Volcano icon by dDara/The Noun Project
Rocket icon by Maxim Kulikov/The Noun Project
Peach icon by Vectorstall/The Noun Project
Dolphin icon by Iconic/The Noun Project
Key icon by Eagle Eye/The Noun Project
Heart icon by Colourcreatype/The Noun Project
Muscle icon by Vectors Market/The Noun Project
Ring icon by Vectors Point/The Noun Project

10 9 8 7 6 5 4 3 2 1

Library of Congress Cataloging-in-Publication
Names: Barrett, Connell, author.
Title: Dating sucks, but you don't / Connell Barrett.
Description: New York, NY : Tiller Press, [2021] | Includes bibliographical references.
Identifiers: LCCN 2020048094 (print) | LCCN 2020048095 (ebook) |
  ISBN 9781982159139 (hardcover) | ISBN 9781982159153 (ebook)
Subjects: LCSH: Dating (Social customs) | Mate selection. | Man-woman
  relationships. | Men—Life skills guides.
Classification: LCC HQ801 .B329 2021 (print) | LCC HQ801 (ebook) | DDC 306.73—dc23

ISBN 978-1-9821-5913-9
ISBN 978-1-9821-5914-6 (pbk)
ISBN 978-1-9821-5915-3 (ebook)

To the memory of my mom, who taught me my ABCs.
To Alex, who let me get close.
And to the magnetic, authentic man you're about to become.

....

CONTENTS

....

INTRODUCTION	What Women *Really* Want	xi
CHAPTER 1	Keeping It Really Real: Radical Authenticity	1
CHAPTER 2	"Your Looks Matter" & Other Dating Myths	17
CHAPTER 3	Your Sucky Love Life Is Your Fault (and That's a Good Thing): Building Core Confidence	31
CHAPTER 4	For Added Value, Add Some Values	47
CHAPTER 5	How to Ignite Romantic Connection	63
CHAPTER 6	Are You Manly Enough to Be Feminine?	87
CHAPTER 7	It's Not You—It's the Halibut You're Holding: How to Get Good at Online Dating	93
CHAPTER 8	You Had Me at Hello: Great First Dates	121
CHAPTER 9	Get Your Head Out of Your Apps: How to Approach and Connect (Part 1)	143
CHAPTER 10	Tools & Techniques: How to Approach and Connect (Part 2)	161
CHAPTER 11	Advanced Ninja Moves	183
CHAPTER 12	You Found That Lovin' Feelin'	193
CHAPTER 13	Consent Is Sexy: How to Date in the #MeToo Era	201
CHAPTER 14	The Secret to Total Confidence & Romantic Connection	215
	Additional Resources	221
	Acknowledgments	227
	Notes	229

CONTENTS

INTRODUCTION / What Women Really Want xi

CHAPTER 1   Keeping It Really Real: Radical Authenticity 1

CHAPTER 2   Your Looks Matter & Other Dating Myths 17

CHAPTER 3   Your Sucky Love Life Is Your Fault,
and That's a Good Thing: Building
Core Confidence 41

CHAPTER 4   For Added Value, Add Some Value 67

CHAPTER 5   How to Ignite Romantic Connection 91

CHAPTER 6   Are You Manly Enough to Be Feminine? 107

CHAPTER 7   If It's Not Fun—It's the Hell of You: Avoiding,
How to Get Good at Online Dating 115

CHAPTER 8   You Had Me at Hello: Great First Dates 131

CHAPTER 9   Get Your Head Out of Your Apps:
How to Approach and Connect (Part 1):
Both & Techniques 149

CHAPTER 10 How to Approach and Connect (Part 2):
Advanced Ninja Moves 159

CHAPTER 11 ...to Found That Loving Realm 193

CHAPTER 12 Chased It, Seen, How to Date
in the Make You Era 201

CHAPTER 13 The Secret to True Confidence &
Romantic Connection 219

CHAPTER 14 Additional Resources 224

Acknowledgments 227

Notes 229

WHAT WOMEN
REALLY WANT

> Most people are other people. Their thoughts are
> someone else's opinions, their lives a mimicry.
> —Oscar Wilde, *De Profundis*; author, playwright, authentic soul[1]

> You're so money and you don't even know it!
> —Trent (Vince Vaughn), *Swingers*[2]

What do women want? It's one of life's most elusive, profound questions, right up there with "Are we alone in the universe?" and "Do dogs name their owners?"

You might think that a man's dating success comes down to looks, height, or money, but those things don't really matter. They're like Jacuzzis—nice to have but way overrated.

So, what do women really want? How can you "get the girl"? The answer comes down to one word: authenticity.

Or to elaborate: Be who you truly are at your core, because women will like you for you.

Lean into being the nice guy, or brainy introvert, or divorced dad that you are. If you embrace authenticity in your love life, then your confidence will skyrocket, you'll get more dates, and you'll soon be sharing your life with a wonderful woman who loves the real you.

I hesitate to give it all away right out of the gate, especially if you haven't yet swiped your credit card and bought this book, but I want to be straight with you. Authenticity is always the answer to finding the woman of your dreams, and I'll go into why in just a bit. But first, ask yourself if any of these dating problems sound familiar:

- You want to approach beautiful women—at your gym, in bars, in cafés, wherever—but something holds you back.
- You get ghosted a lot.
- You're often banished to the friend zone by women you're into.
- You're not sure how to flirt or how to keep conversations going, and when you do talk to women you're attracted to, you tend to run out of things to say.
- You swipe and swipe on dating apps, but you get few (if any) quality matches—and the matches you get rarely turn into dates.
- You perhaps do go on some dates—but not with the kinds of women you'd love to meet.
- You haven't had a great girlfriend in a while, and sometimes you feel lonely.
- You have a scarcity of dating options—at least, ones you're excited about.
- You've settled before and are likely to do so again.
- You feel that cool, cute girls are out of your league, that somehow you're "not enough" for them.
- As the years creep by, you cling to the hope of finding that one incredible woman to share your life with, but you fear it may never happen.

Do any of those frustrations sound familiar? If so, I totally get it. I battled all of those issues before I learned how to fix every one of them. (Hell, I didn't just live in the friend zone—I owned a condo there.) And I think it's just plain wrong when a great guy lacks self-confidence and doesn't have the dating life he deserves. It shouldn't be this way.

The great news? You can change this. Because women like you. A lot.

It's true! They dig you. Lots of women find you attractive, cool, and even sexy. I don't know you personally, of course, but I'm guessing that you're sincere and smart. You like and respect women, viewing them as people, not bedpost notches. You may not fully see it, but you're a good guy with a lot to offer. And that makes you a helluva catch.

Now, I can almost hear you: "That sounds good, Mr. Dating Coach, but I'm just not the guy attractive girls go for." You might feel that you're not handsome enough or cool enough. Or maybe you think you don't know the right words women want to hear. Something seems to be missing, right?

I beg to differ. There's nothing missing within you. In fact, focusing on your so-called shortcomings *is* the problem. Self-doubt is your enemy. It tamps down the confidence you need to approach that gorgeous woman who's two feet away from you. It keeps you from asking your crush out on a date. It's the reason you run out of things to say. And self-doubt is why you're afraid that you'll end up settling—either for a woman you're not that into, or for being alone.

But here's the truth: You are enough. Desirable women love nice, normal guys like you—once they meet the real, authentic you.

If you don't believe me, let me tell you about Ken.

NICE GUYS FINISH FIRST

When I became his dating coach, Ken was pushing thirty and had never even kissed a girl. But he had a lot going for him: a good teaching job at a college, a silly sense of humor (he's a big fan of knock-knock jokes), and a deep knowledge of ancient Greek literature. Most guys can quote Homer Simpson. Ken can quote Homer's *Odyssey*.

But he's also introverted, stocky, and on the shorter side (think Jonah Hill), and he told me something during our first meeting that echoes what many single men feel: "I'm just not attractive to women." In other words: I'm not enough.

"We do not see things as they are," Anaïs Nin wrote in her novel *Seduction of the Minotaur*, "we see them as we are."[3] A man views his love life through the lens of his identity—the story he tells himself about who he is. My job? Help Ken—and guys like him—change his story, and thereby change his world.

Ken had just read *The Game*, Neil Strauss's 2005 book[4] about the pickup-artist community, and he'd bought into the premise that you "game" women by adopting a false persona and using scripted lines. "There's a better way," I told him. "Girls like you for you, the real guy inside. But you're hiding that guy. Don't wear a mask. Show women the real you."

I also told him that introverted guys like us (I'm a card-carrying introvert) have a dating edge over extroverts because we tend to be great listeners and deeply self-aware, traits that women value.

He was a bit skeptical but agreed to try it out. The two of us spent a weekend hitting up bars and lounges in New York City. As he chatted with more and more women, Ken's slumped shoulders straightened, his voice grew louder, and his laugh began to boom.

He went up to these women not with "smooth" pickup lines but with awesomely dorky knock-knock jokes. He followed up with deep conversations about Plato and Aristotle. Hardly your usual bar banter. At one point, I had Ken approach a curvaceous NYU grad student who wore cat-eye glasses. Ken's a karaoke nut, so as his "opener" he sang the first few lines of Prince's "Purple Rain." As he serenaded her, she joined right in, and within seconds they were holding hands, doing a duet. A few minutes later, she snatched Ken's iPhone, punched in her number, and said, "You'd better text me. I love nerdy guys."

As Ken and I walked to the next bar, he said, "A girl has never looked at me like that or asked me out," referring to Cat-Eye Glasses. "It was so fun and simple." Bingo.

Later that night, on a rooftop bar, Ken saw a Gwyneth Paltrow look-alike in a yellow dress and went for it. She smiled when he approached, and they began talking. Like him, she loved classics books. He took her hand and led her to the bar for drinks. Then he made his move: He leaned in and up (she had three inches on him). Cue: full make-out.

I almost looked away because it was such a personal moment. I'd never knowingly witnessed someone's first-ever kiss. But I couldn't peel my eyes off of Ken, who seemed like a different guy from a couple days earlier. He'd awakened his most charismatic, confident self—which as it turned out is equal parts good-hearted dork and bold badass. It was the real man buried beneath layers of doubt and flawed dating advice. Six months later, he had a great girlfriend.

Ken changed that night—at least in terms of how he saw himself in relation to women. He transformed from Mr. Not Enough to Authentic Ken. And when you awaken your true self, you awaken a new dating life.

WHAT THIS BOOK WILL TEACH YOU

In this book, I'll show you everything I taught Ken, so that you can take new actions—starting tomorrow—that lead to a similar transformation. You'll get the essential tools you need to land a great girlfriend and do it as your most confident, authentic self. You're going to learn . . .

- How to attract the girlfriend you always wanted, even if you're not tall, rich, or great-looking
- How to become confident and magnetic as the awesome guy you already are
- How to defeat fear and approach women in a charming way
- How to get more quality matches on dating apps
- How to escape the friend zone
- How to keep conversations going with women and never "run out of things to say"

You'll also learn . . .

- How to spark attraction on first dates
- The "cheat codes" for texting
- The best way to move in for the kiss—in a way that women love
- The ten dating-app openers that get girls writing you back
- How to cut way down on ghosting
- How to do all of this as a gentleman who respects women— with zero sketchy "pickup artist" moves

No matter how big or small your dating problems, I can help. If your love life is flatlining, consider this book to be your defibrillator. (Clear!) If you just want to upgrade in a couple areas—more Tinder matches, say, or knowing how to make the first move—I've got you covered as well.

What does this all mean for you? One day soon you'll wake up with your dream girlfriend next to you—a lover and best friend who sees your true heart and mind—and you'll think, *I've become the man I always wanted to be.*

Plus, a great dating life flows into other areas, like ripples on a pond. Since you're generally happier, your fitness improves, your social connections deepen, and your career can reach new heights. So what are you waiting for?

WHY LISTEN TO ME?

Because I can help almost any man transform his dating life. I'm an international dating coach for men, the founder of Dating Transformation, and a coach for the dating app The League. You may have seen me on *The Today Show*, *Access Hollywood*, or CNN, or read my advice in *Maxim*, *Playboy*, or AskMen. I spent nearly a decade training with the world's best dating and self-development experts, and over the last eight years I've coached thousands of men in a dozen countries, helping regular guys land their dream partners. In 2019, Datezie named me New York City's best male dating coach.

But on a more personal level, I can solve any dating problem because I've *had* every dating problem. Like Ken, for years I felt unattractive to women. When I finally met the rare girl who wanted me, I married her—and she dumped me nine weeks later. (It was over so fast that we could have fought for custody of the wedding cake.)

As I drove away from her house in my red Honda Civic—the backseat loaded with unwrapped wedding gifts to be returned for store credit—I felt rejected by an entire gender. I would soon hit my low point. In the years that followed, I nearly went broke going to prostitutes. In my mind, I was unworthy of women, so I had to pay them to be with me. While my friends were getting engaged and coupling up, I was in seedy hotels handing strangers envelopes full of cash, fearing arrest and feeling shame—all for scraps of intimacy. My self-esteem had hit a new low.

I remember the moment when I knew things had to change. I was in a Starbucks on a Sunday afternoon when I saw a beautiful brunette in a denim miniskirt who was sitting by herself. I felt I had to meet her, so I walked over, got within a few feet . . . and said nothing. I even circled her table a couple of times like a frightened shark, but a powerful inner force kept me from talking to her. I was afraid of getting shot down, and I worried that "hitting on her" would make me seem creepy. She finished her iced coffee and left, and I told myself, *You suck. There goes yet another girl you won't be dating.*

It was at that point that I'd had enough. I decided to embark on a quest to learn what really works with women. I hired classy dating coaches and sleazy pickup artists. I approached thousands of women and went on hundreds of dates. It wasn't easy—at first, I was rejected more than a Jehovah's Witness. But in time I cracked the code of romantic connection. The more authentically I presented myself, the more women liked me for me.

Crazy things started happening. I began attracting models, actresses, dream-girls-next-door, and one particularly memorable cable-news "money honey," as she described herself. (There's just something about a woman discussing annual percentage yields, amirite?) Instead of hearing "Let's be friends" on dates, I began hearing "Let's go to your place." Once, in London, a lovely Brit I'd just met at an upscale lounge shushed me mid-sentence and said, "You have ten seconds to kiss me. Nine, eight, seven . . ." Many women have asked me to be their boyfriend.

And if I can do it, you can, too. Since becoming a coach, I've helped countless guys like you all over the world get similar results, taking their love lives to new heights. My training methods are pretty simple. Through a combination of Skype and one-on-one in-person sessions, I teach my clients how to be more confident, how to approach with charm, how to get more matches and dates on Tinder and the apps—and how to land a great girlfriend.

My point? You're in good hands.

WHAT THIS BOOK IS

You're holding a step-by-step road map to help you build confidence, attract wonderful women, and ultimately find a great partner—all as the authentic you. Franz Kafka once wrote to a friend, "A book must be the axe for the frozen sea inside of us."[5] This book is your axe.

Yes, this is about meeting your dream woman. But it's also about becoming a better man. My view is, when you master dating, you master life. Because you approach women the same way you need to approach the world—with vulnerability, courage, and love.

At the end of most chapters, I'll give you missions to help guide you on your path to unstoppable confidence and romantic connection. The missions are a lot of fun, but a few—such as approaching women—may seem scary. Please do them to the best of your ability. While I'm proud of the teachings I've laid out here, reading by itself isn't enough to get you the dating life you desire, nor will doing what you've been doing.

You must take new actions. What you've done up until now hasn't worked.

And you must face your fears and do what feels uncomfortable. If this book is an axe, you're the one who has to swing it.

I'm not worried. The fact that you're reading this means that you're a man of action. And let me say that I have massive respect for you because I feel like I know you. I was once searching for answers, too. Most single guys live lives of quiet dating desperation. Not you. You're not settling. I honor that, which is why I'll give you the tools to make new shifts, adopt new behaviors, and build a new love life.

WHAT THIS BOOK IS NOT

You won't be reading the same old tips. There's an ocean of bad dating advice out there. Apart from the superficial, sleazy clickbait that litters the internet ("One Weird Trick to Get Her Into Bed . . ."), most so-called dating experts fail you. They're either too tactical, too focused on "seduction," or both. This book strikes the right balance of mindset and field-tested techniques, revealing both the inner values and the social dynamics that lead to romantic connection.

Oh, and not for nothing, I like and respect women. I teach cutting-edge personal development, not creepy "seduction" tricks. I'm a normal guy, not a peacocking, button-pushing "player." (Besides, loud shirts and shiny medallions clash with my ginger hair.)

And if you're suspicious of self-help books—well, so am I. But this is one of the good ones. I'm here to give you fresh, practical, right-minded advice. You'll find no vague, woo-woo language about "positive thinking," nor will you encounter cheesy acronyms ("Use my S.U.C.C.E.S.S. System . . ."). I find that stuff super D.O.U.C.H.E.Y.

SEIZE THE DATE!

Before he became a great philosopher, the Greek Stoic Epictetus was born a slave. (His master once twisted the young man's iron-clad leg until bones broke.) Epictetus decided to become more. His handbook the *Enchiridion* includes the wise words, "First say to yourself what you would be; and then do what you have to do."[6]

I think that you know what you have to do. It's time to become the man you always wanted to be in the area of dating.

This is important. Don't put off fixing your love life. Procrastination is a creditor who charges steep interest in the form of loneliness and low confidence. It's time for action.

You are enough. You definitely don't suck. And when you have self-confidence and deep connections with women, neither does dating. Because women already like you. They just have to meet the real you.

So carpe date 'em. Seize the date!

DATING IN A POST-COVID WORLD

I'm writing this in the autumn of 2020 when much of the U.S. is still in coronavirus lockdown. Many of America's singles are a lot like teens stuck in summer school: horny, bored, and trapped inside.

This book is a dating guide for a normal(-ish) world. By the time you read this, I hope COVID-19 has been defeated by a powerful vaccine—preferably one that's bourbon-flavored and can be imbibed with ice. But if the crisis (or a future catastrophe) is still wreaking havoc where you live, adjust your dating actions accordingly and ignore any advice I offer that seems untenable. For example, if you go on a socially distanced date, you won't be using the tips I give in Chapter 5 about being physically expressive. And if there's a new outbreak near you, please don't visit a crowded bar to do the approach missions from chapters 9 and 10. Protect your own health and that of others.

As awful as the pandemic has been, I foresee some silver linings to your love life. Singles have returned to the nineties—the 1890s. Old-timey courtship is back because it now takes so much more effort to safely date someone. Fewer people are bed-hopping. Men and women are actually (gasp!) getting to know each other before becoming physical. This is a good thing.

I'm all for fun flings and giving yourself multiple romantic options, but dating is ultimately about finding that one fantastic woman for a deep, committed relationship. When we're looking for love in a post-COVID world, I hope courtship and connection stay in vogue.

KEEPING IT REALLY REAL

RADICAL AUTHENTICITY

> Be the person your dog thinks you are.
> —Ricky Gervais, on Twitter[1]

....

I t was the late 2000s in New York City, and a wavy-haired investment banker was stealing my girl right in front of me. And she was letting him.

Today, as a dating coach, I can handle this sort of situation. But when it happened more than a decade ago—on the first night I ever went out to approach women, no less—I panicked.

It had been a great July night in the city. The rooftop lounge in the shadow of the Empire State Building was hopping, and I was clicking with Kelly, a witty actress with ocean-blue eyes. I'd approached her an hour before, and we had an easy chemistry. Our conversation went deeper than bar banter. We were being real with each other, even revealing our nerdy nicknames from grade school. (I was the chubby redhead they called "Mack Truck," and she was the flat-chested girl dubbed "Mosquito Bites.") We hadn't kissed yet, but it felt like it was only a matter of time.

Kelly knew I was a journalist out that night with my friend. What she didn't know was that my friend was a renowned dating coach, and that I was part of a boot camp he was running to teach men how to meet and attract women. Nor did she know that before that evening, I'd never once approached a woman cold. Nor did she know that earlier I was so anxious, so afraid of rejection, that I'd gotten the dry heaves in a men's-room stall.

Why did I pony up $2,500 for a weekend with a dating expert? Because I was just done. I was done hearing, "I only see you as a friend." I was done feeling lonely. I was done seeing head-turning girls in bars, parks, or at the gym and being too afraid to talk to them. I was done watching cooler guys attract the women I ached to date. I was done seeing my friends couple up while I was left behind. I was done paying escorts for sex. I was done feeling like half a man. I was done settling. And I was just plain done.

So it was thrilling to find myself vibing with Kelly, the coolest, prettiest woman in the place. "I'll get us more drinks," I told her. When I came back with our vodka sodas, she was ringed by three Wall Street bros. The handsome, wavy-haired guy in the middle had her twirling her chestnut locks and giggling.

I assumed that on my return, Kelly and I would pick up where we left off. Wrong. "Here's your drink," I said. She took it without breaking eye contact with Wavy Hair. It was like I wasn't there. Minutes ago, I had been her date. Now I was her waiter.

"Umm, maybe we should go downstairs?" I asked feebly. She ignored me. Wavy Hair's wingmen closed the circle, turned their backs to me, and boxed me out. My shoulders slumped. All my adult life, charismatic guys like this dated the kinds of women I wanted to be with—and now one of them was stealing the rare girl who liked me.

I found my coach at the bar and filled him in on the situation. I'd read in online "seduction" forums about the various ways to handle the AMOG—the socially dominant alpha male of the group. "What's my move?" I asked. Make her jealous by talking to other women? Decimate the guy's confidence with the perfect barb? Give him a knuckle sandwich?

"Just go take her away from him," my coach said.

"What do you mean?" I asked, sopping sweat off my forehead.

"She was with you, and you were hitting it off, right?" I nodded. "She likes you, but she wants to see if you're gonna go after what you want. It's survival of the fittest. She's leaving the bar tonight with either you or him. Who's it gonna be?"

"I want it to be me," I said.

"Then assert your ideal outcome. If she was your girlfriend and was flirting with another guy in front of you, would you just give up?"

"Fuck no," I said, feeling something inside of me stir. "I'd march over there and stop it."

"Then go," he said. "Take her back."

"What should I say?"

"Don't overthink it. Speak your deepest truth."

Adrenaline flowing, I beelined toward Kelly, broke into their circle, took her hand, and commanded, "Come with me. Now." She said, "Bye, guyyyyys," as I yanked her away and led her to a nearby bench. The investment wankers didn't utter a word and didn't follow. I was in charge now.

Not sure what to say, I reminded myself: *Speak your deepest truth*. The right words came. "I like you," I told Kelly. "You're smart and soulful and sexy, but it's not cool to try to make me jealous."

I half expected her to splash me in the face with her Ketel One, but she leaned closer, twirling a tendril of hair, biting her lip. I realized, *Holy shit— this is turning her on*. "You just yanked me away from those guys like you own me," she said, with a hint of a smile. Another test, I realized. She wanted to see if I would apologize for my bold move.

I didn't back down. I'd never felt so confident, so strong. "I don't own you," I said. "I barely know you—but I want to know you better. And when I want something, I go after it. And I want you."

Until that moment, I'd never made a woman swoon. I leaned in, we kissed, and were together for the rest of the night, which ended at my apartment.

The next morning, I stared in awe at Kelly as she slept. I lightly poked her shoulder to make sure she was really there. I'd never had someone this beautiful in my bed before.

I felt fantastic but unsteady. I'd always thought I was a nerdy, introverted loser who had to settle for less in his love life. Now I was asking new questions: *Can you really just walk up to women, be yourself, and they'll like you? If this is possible, what else is possible?*

Kelly shifted position in her sleep and threw her long, tan leg over mine. As it turns out, plenty more is possible.

PUTTING THE "AWE" IN AUTHENTICITY

In this chapter, I'll give you a whole new way to gain confidence, become more attractive to women, and transform your dating life. I'll also share five simple steps you can take to put you on the path to finding your dream partner.

And don't worry. You won't have to vanquish a bunch of Wall Street bros to bring a wonderful woman into your life. My story was just meant to illustrate some of the essential values—courage, taking action, telling deep truths—that will improve your romantic fortunes.

These features comprise a dating philosophy I call Radical Authenticity. It means being fully grounded in who you are at your core—your deepest, truest, most awesome self—and then putting that amazing guy in charge of your dating life. It means speaking honest thoughts and taking honest action, all while leaning into what makes you distinctly you. It's a potent approach to dating that unlocks the door to a fulfilling, connected love life.

MEET THE HERO OF YOUR STORY— AND THE VILLAIN

So why did Kelly choose me that night, instead of a richer, handsomer, more outgoing guy? Because the courage and vulnerability I showed elevated me in her eyes. She saw more value in me than in my competition.

A few days after that evening, I relayed the story to a friend, who said, "That doesn't sound anything like you." Actually, when I told Kelly "I want you," I'd never felt *more* like me. The insecure, self-doubting dweeb I had been presenting to the women of the world was the impostor. The candid, confident man was the real me.

Although he was new to me in the area of dating, that confident guy had been a regular fixture in other parts of my life. I had a kick-ass magazine job, a fantastic circle of friends, and I could shoot 77 on the golf course. In these arenas, I was a man of mastery. But ask me to approach a *guh-guh-guh*-girl and I morphed into a jittery, armpit-stained loser who'd quake in the presence of this mysterious species called the female. Why the dichotomy? Why was I Dr. Jekyll and Mr. Hide from Girls?

As my years studying dating have revealed, it's because you, me, everyone—we all have dual selves. A Higher Self and a Lower Self.

Your Higher Self is the hero of your life. In any arena that brings you joy, fulfillment, and results, your Higher Self is in charge. He's confident, focused, and totally authentic. He's you operating at full potential. The job you love, the biceps you've sculpted, the great kid you're raising—it's the superhero inside of you running the show.

But every superhero has an archvillain, a mustache-twirling bad guy. And that's your Lower Self. This is the fearful, doubtful part of you who's been botching up your love life. It's the voice that whispers, *Don't approach her— she's out of your league.* The pain and frustrations you've felt—from settling for the friend zone to feeling unworthy of quality women—that's all the fault of your Lower Self.

Higher Self = You at Your Best
Lower Self = You at Your Worst

I'm a *Star Wars* nerd, and I love the original trilogy because our hero learns that he had Jedi powers all along—he just had to channel them. Your Higher Self is the Jedi within you. Or, as my client Ken put it, in analogy form: "Authenticity is to dating as the Force is to Luke Skywalker."

We can't forget who the bad guy is, though. There's great power in understanding your enemy. On the first day of their training, I have my clients give their Lower Selves a name—a nickname to make them cringe. Freddie, an attorney in his late thirties, came to me because he would feel a lot of stress and fear when he wanted to say hello to an attractive stranger—what's called "approach anxiety." His hands would shake at the thought of walking up to a woman and saying hi, so he named his Lower Self "Frightened Freddie." Nick, a jazz musician who was struggling to get matches and dates on Tinder, named his enemy within "No Nuts Nick." Me? My Lower Self is "Connie," a grade-school nickname that I hated and that now reminds me of the pain my Lower Self caused.

Next, I have my clients recall a specific moment of awesomeness—a time when they felt fulfilled, confident, and present. These mental snapshots can really be anything, from crossing the finish line at a marathon, to playing electric guitar in a band, to laughing with close friends or family. Then they give that guy a name, because he's their Higher Self—and he's capable of doing incredible things. "Frightened Freddie" became "Frederick the Great," a guy who could soon successfully approach women almost anywhere. "No Nuts Nick" transformed into "Nick Summers," whose phone would eventually be blowing up with Tinder dates. My Higher Self's name? It's so stupid that it's brilliant: I went from "Connie" to "Connell Fuckin Barrett," a bold man of action. (You can call me CFB for short.)

Your Lower Self contains all the pain and doubt that contributed to your sucky dating life. But your Higher Self has bottomless confidence and can get lots of dates, and in time connect with one incredible woman. To be clear, your Higher Self is not a persona or a mask. Nor is he you after a couple of stiff whiskeys. He's the true inner you buried beneath layers of doubts and fears—that priceless, gleaming diamond encased by worthless igneous rock.

This book is about how to drill down to that Higher Self and put him in charge of your dating life. It's time to hand your Lower Self a cigarette and blindfold and let your Higher Self run your love life.

RADICAL AUTHENTICITY

When you channel your authentic, real self and project that guy in your dating life, a woman feels two very powerful things: attraction and trust. She is attracted to you because it takes confidence to unapologetically be yourself—and confidence is intoxicating to women. She also begins to trust you as she sees that you're being honest. As a single woman, she's heard more lies than a polygraph expert. When you're authentic, you signal to her that you're a guy she can finally trust.

And when there's both attraction and trust, you create a real connection.

Being authentic is powerful in any walk of life, but in dating it's rare, making it ten times more potent. When you put your real self on the line, you stand out. Not only is authenticity what women crave—it creates a vibe that's more fun, connecting, and exciting, and thus makes your dating life even better.

Here are seven benefits that Radical Authenticity brings to your life:

1. **You Have More Confidence:** When you align your thoughts, words, and actions with your most pure self, you feel free. You stand taller, talk louder, and become comfortable in your own skin. "When you stop hiding parts of yourself from other people, you'll find you feel more confident in who you are," Charlie Houpert, founder of the popular YouTube channel Charisma on Command, told the *New York Times* in 2019.[2] And when you're more confident . . .

2. **You Become Magnetic to Women:** Not all of them, of course, but lots more than you might think. They have a sixth sense for a man who knows himself and believes in himself. It takes anvil-sized cojones to be real and vulnerable in dating, and women appreciate it and like it. All other things equal, the amount of attraction she feels is in direct proportion to how authentic you are—thinking, speaking, and acting from a true place.

3. **You Create Genuine Connections:** As best-selling author Brené Brown explains in a TED Talk, "Authenticity is the daily practice of letting go of who we think we're supposed to be and embracing who we are."[3] This not only makes you more attractive but allows you to connect at a deeper, more genuine level.

4. **You Know Your Worth:** When you're authentic, you send a powerful message to yourself and to your date: I am enough. And when you know you're enough, fear of rejection subsides.

5. **You Know What to Say:** Many guys struggle to find the "right words" when talking to women. If you feel your words are insufficient, it's often because you fear that *you're* insufficient. When you're authentic, a powerful paradox kicks in. You stop straining for the right thing to say and simply speak freely—and that's when the right words come.

6. **You Elevate Other Areas of Your Life:** When you fix your dating problems, you free up untold gigabytes of mental RAM, helping you to excel in other important areas, like your fitness, your friendships, and your career. Plus, the authenticity that allows you to crush it in dating will carry over into these other areas of your life, fueling your success and fulfillment. And studies show that authentic people are fitter, healthier, have high self-esteem, and are less likely to be depressed.

7. **Your Dating Life Stops Sucking:** When your authentic self is running the show, a whole new world opens up. Imagine your impressed buddies saying, *You seem different. What's changed, man?* Imagine women you've only known as "just friends" chasing *you* for a change. Imagine finally *enjoying* dating.

There's science to back up the transformational power that authenticity can have on your love life. According to a 2019 Western Sydney University study called "Be Yourself: Authenticity as a Long-Term Mating Strategy," being an honest, authentic dater makes you more attractive to potential partners, compared to those who "play games" (acting hard to get, not replying to texts, etc.).[4] Also, a 1998 study from Leiden University in the Netherlands suggests that being real is hard to fake and that trying to fake it backfires. False flattery can create the so-called "slime effect,"[5] making the faker appear unlikable and manipulative—and nobody is attracted to that.

THE MASKS MEN WEAR

Unfortunately, few men date from a truly authentic place. Most guys wear a kind of mask around women, playing the part of the People Pleaser, or the Bad Boy, or the Pickup Artist. They do this because they suspect that women won't like them for who they are. It's a psychological defense mechanism, so that in case they get ghosted, they can rationalize it as, *She didn't really reject me because she didn't meet the* real *me*. But shielding yourself from rejection also shields you from connection.

The worst mask of all? Unworthy Man, the guy who avoids putting himself out there, fearing the sting of rejection. When wearing this mask, a guy has the mindset that *Dating reminds me that I'm not enough, and that hurts, so I won't date*. This leads to short-term relief but at a long-term cost: loneliness, settling, social isolation, and in extreme cases misogyny, depression, and thoughts of suicide. To borrow a phrase from John Updike, this mask eats into the face.

But it's only a mask, just like all the others. You can remove it at any time.

THE LYING GAME

I wore many masks over the years. For example, take my interactions with a woman named Lisa. I was way into her. She was the perfect combination of smart and sexy and quick with one-liners. After our first date, I was schoolboy-smitten, all but scribbling "Connell + Lisa" on a spiral notebook.

But I felt out of my league with her—a Toledo Mud Hen playing in Yankee Stadium. What would a bright bombshell like her see in a bookish nerd like me? She was into scuba and hiking, so on our second date I pretended to be the rugged, outdoorsy guy I thought she wanted. Which is to say, I made a bunch of shit up. I told her I was studying to get my pilot's license (lie), loved skydiving (double lie), and swam with sharks in the Caribbean (double-dog lie). I have a terrible poker face, and as I spun these tall tales, my forehead became a Slip 'N Slide of sweat. After that date, she friend-zoned me, of course. Because when you feel unworthy and pretend to be someone you're not, women can tell. Their B.S. detectors are more finely tuned than the Richter scale.

Yet when you're authentic, you're at ease, making you more confident and attractive. Also, you give women a singular experience. After all, you're not one in a million. You're one in seven billion. It's the difference between a watered-down wine spritzer and a strong Scotch.

Women want to catch a buzz on the good stuff—the top-shelf, 80-proof, barrel-aged you.

If you're a book-loving nerd like me, fly that banner high. If you're a hipster, rock that goatee. If you're a single dad, lean into it and talk about your kid. We all have types, and plenty of women love nerds and hipsters. As for single dads, being a parent is the most important job on the planet—and women like a guy with a cool job. (My ex used to go to Central Park with her girlfriends to, as she said, "scope out the DILFs.")

It takes courage to put your real self out there, so when a woman realizes she's meeting the genuine article—and if she likes your type—she'll be super into you. Your natural chemistry will Spinal Tap up to 11.

(Oh, a year after blowing me off, Lisa gave me another shot—with a very different outcome. More on that in Chapter 8.)

THE FIVE PILLARS OF RADICAL AUTHENTICITY

What makes a Radically Authentic man? In a word, he's "congruent," meaning in harmony with himself. His thoughts, words, and actions align with his core values. He listens to his gut. He follows his passions. He's expressive, less filtered than most men. He's kind, compassionate, and appreciative of life. He's empathetic to others' feelings, but doesn't change who he is based on his environment. He's a straight-shooting, decent dude.

Here are the five pillars of Radical Authenticity:

1. **Honesty:** Never lie to women and never present a false front. Share your sense of humor, your points of view, your passions. The more honest you are, the more you accept your authentic self.

2. **Vulnerability:** Let your flaws, fears, and mistakes show while fully owning them. It takes strength to be vulnerable, and women love strong men.

3. **Taking Action:** Align your actions with your words and values. As Shakespeare wrote, "Action is eloquence."

4. **Kindness:** It's the thing women want most in a guy, according to a 2019 survey of 64,000 single women conducted by the University of Göttingen in Germany and the female health app Clue.[6] So be nice.

5. **Growing and Giving:** In dating and in life, the more you grow, the more you give—and the more you give, the more women want to give back.

EUDAIMONIA? YOU DA MAN!

Authenticity is about taking full responsibility for yourself and your life, and its use has deep roots. The word "authentic" comes from the Greek *authentikos*, meaning, "To act in one's own authority." To be authentic means to be your own authority and to act in accordance with your deepest thoughts and feelings instead of blindly reacting to your environment.

The phrase "know thyself" was first used some three thousand years ago by the Oracle at Delphi, and later by great thinkers like Socrates, Plato, and Aristotle. As for Aristotle, well, he was wrong about a lot. He called slavery natural and thought eels sprang from mud and rainwater. But he did give us an elegant concept called eudaimonia.

Roughly translated as "human flourishing," eudaimonia (pronounced "you-dy-moh-nee-uh") means to live in harmony with your inherent character. In his *Nicomachean Ethics*, Aristotle argued that everyone is born with singular gifts, and that only by becoming your best self can you truly live a good life. In other words, you're here to pursue your potential—to become a great husband or the world's finest whittler or the forty-seventh member of the Beach Boys. The best way to be a person, Aristotle said, is to be the best person you can be.

What does all this high philosophy have to do with gettin' girls? Well, it boils down to value. Simply put, authenticity equals value, and value equals attraction.

That Scarlett Johansson look-alike you're pining over? You're attracted to her because you see value in her wit, her curves, her voice—not to mention the potential for love and companionship. For her to be into you, she must see relevant value that you can bring to her life. Attraction is a trade. Before you trade sweet nothings, you have to trade value.

By definition, any authentic thing is valuable because it's real, rare, and has utility. An authentic Picasso sells for millions at Sotheby's. An authentic voice cuts through the bullshit at a sales meeting. An authentic tech brand connects with its geeky customers. And an authentic man is magnetic to women on a dating landscape rife with liars, players, and pretenders.

Authenticity = value and value = attraction

The night I met Kelly, I removed my mask and showed her an authentic man who offered her value and who could be vulnerable, brave, and honest. It's what created the connection.

Aristotle called that a "virtuous man." I call that your Higher Self. And Radical Authenticity is how you summon your inner superhero to transform your dating life.

Authenticity is king, connection is queen—and forever may they reign.

CHAPTER 1 MISSIONS

Five Steps to Becoming Radically Authentic

1. **Name Your Lower Self**
   It's time to know your enemy. Give your Lower Self a name.
   It could be a childhood nickname you despised, or a de-

scription that encapsulates your biggest dating problem: "Anxious Aaron," "Not-Confident Chris," "Frankie Friend Zone." (Alliteration is fun but not required.) The trick? Choose a name that makes you feel profound disgust. Link pain to your Lower Self, so that leaving behind this loser becomes a must.

2. **Name Your Higher Self**
   Name your best, most awesomely authentic you. If it helps, recall a moment when you felt powerful and in the zone—the speech you aced, the dance contest you won, that woman you approached who loved it. What's that guy's name? My clients' nicknames include "Badass Brett," "Caesar the Great," and "Confident Curt." Steal mine, if you like: "[First name] Fuckin [Last name]." The name you choose should make you feel great. It represents the real you—the guy who's gonna take your dating life to new heights.

3. **Apply Your New Golden Rule**
   To become more authentic, adopt this as your dating mantra: "What I'm thinking and feeling is what I'm saying and doing." Start living by this credo to make you more congruent and authentic.

   A couple caveats: Don't say crude, vulgar things. A Radically Authentic man tells it like it is, yes. But he's also kind and aware of how he makes others feel. And don't mistake honesty for "venting." Authentic speech is not a license to bitch and moan. Be an open book, not an open wound.

4. **Choose a Passion Project**
   The more you grow as a man, the more attractive you become to women. Choose a self-improvement project that excites you. Reading this book counts, but go further. Take a cooking class, or start learning a new language, or volunteer with underprivileged children. This is not only good for the soul.

It gives you great stuff to talk about on dates. Women love a man who has passion for life, and who's always evolving.

Speaking of growing, here's a bonus tip: Don't compare yourself to other guys. Compare yourself to the guy you were yesterday and be 1 percent better than him today.

5. **Remind Yourself Every Day . . .**
You. Are. Enough. So be authentic—women like you for the real you. And they can't like him until they meet him.

SO WHAT HAVE WE LEARNED?

....

- You have dual selves: your Lower Self and your Higher Self. When you put your best, most authentic you (your Higher Self) in charge of your dating life, great things will happen.
- Radical Authenticity is the key to romantic connection because it gives women two things they crave: attraction and trust.
- Authenticity = value and value = attraction.
- Aristotle knew human behavior, but he had a lot to learn about eels.

⚡ BONUS TIP ⚡

HOW TO BE "COOL"
....

Some guys think you attract women by being chicly unengaged and mysterious. You know, "cool." But most women don't want cool. They want real.

I'm shamelessly uncool. A total dork. I'm introverted. I love bad movies and dad jokes. I spontaneously sing Broadway show tunes in daily life (with jazz hands). I take classes in coin magic. (Coin magic!) Hardly the hallmarks of a ladies' man.

But when you're uncool without apology, you're free to be you—which is *super cool*. And women who like your brand of uncool will see a twin spirit, which heightens connection. "You're so weird," my future girlfriend said on our second date. "As weird as me."

I've tried being old-school cool, but the proverbial biker jacket just doesn't fit me. The real me is a nice, nerdy redhead from the Midwest.

If you're uncool, own it. And that makes you really cool.

On a final note, make sure you . . . Hey, what's that in your ear? Why, it's a silver dollar!

CHAPTER 2

"YOUR LOOKS MATTER" & OTHER DATING MYTHS

Nobody knows anything.[1]
—William Goldman; screenwriter, Oscar winner, truth teller

....

S tart by approaching those two women," I told my new client, Jason, as we walked into a West Hollywood lounge. "Show me what you can do."

As a dating coach, I frequently play wingman for guys in bars and clubs, and I like to start a night out by assessing a client's social skills. When he talks to women, does his tone project confidence or fear? Does he make eye contact or stare at his shoelaces? Does he stand tall or slouch? I'm looking for behavioral blind spots that may be hurting his chances for romance.

A physically fit, wealthy doctor in his forties, Jason (Higher Self name: "Conan the Barbarian") walked over to two women—a brunette and a redhead—who were both drinking dirty martinis. "Hi," he said, handing them his black-and-gold business card. "I'm a plastic surgeon—for celebrities."

The women seemed confused. Was he looking for new clients—a chin to lift, a tummy to tuck? The redhead self-consciously covered her nose.

Then they realized: This was his "pickup line." They looked at each other and laughed—more *at* him than with him. After a couple minutes of conversation, the brunette said, "Nice meeting you," code for "Not a chance, dude." They left. Approach rejected.

I told Jason why the women headed for the (Hollywood) hills. "You were trying to impress them, and it turned them off," I said. "When you try too hard to impress a woman, it has the opposite effect. It comes across as overcompensating and tells her that you're not at her level—that you're beneath her. And nobody wants to date beneath themselves."

I recognized that Jason had his head up his assets, buying into the myth that the road to a woman's heart is traveled in a Lamborghini. In reality, having cash or a cool job is a nice bonus in the eyes of women, but it doesn't ignite attraction.

The idea that women only want to date rich men is one of several myths that many guys believe. There are other big ones, such as looks and height. "The biggest thing guys get wrong is the three sixes," fellow dating coach Brian Pippard told me, and no, he's not referring to Satanic worship. "They think women only want guys who make six figures, have six-pack abs, and who are six feet or taller. But what women want is a solid man who values and enjoys himself, who's healthily masculine, and expressive."

Buying into a dating myth can hurt you in a couple of key ways. It can compel you to make the wrong move, lowering your standing in women's eyes (such as Jason flashing his business card as his "opener"). It can also disempower you, so you fail to take the right actions—say, not approaching a woman who you think is out of your league.

Let's take a sledgehammer to some debilitating myths. Here are ten of the biggest misconceptions that hurt your dating results, and ten ways to fix them.

MYTH: Your Looks Matter
TRUTH: Looks Are Way Overrated

Hey, if you have chiseled, Hemsworthian features, good on you. But take it from a guy who's dated some beautiful women despite resembling a Weasley brother: Your looks don't matter all that much—unless you make them matter.

If you stop and think, you'll find that the old Joe Jackson song "Is She

Really Going Out with Him?" rings true. How often have you seen a head-turning woman with a regular-looking guy? Lots, I'll bet. There are many high-profile examples, too, from past and present. Arthur Miller and Marilyn Monroe. Lyle Lovett and Julia Roberts. Pete Davidson and Half of Hollywood.

I used to buy into the whole "looks matter" myth, which is partially why I married a woman I wasn't in love with. I wanted to be single and date around, but I felt I wasn't attractive enough to do that, so I settled. And she rightly dumped me nine weeks later.

When I started hiring coaches and getting some good wingmen, I met tons of not-hot guys—chubby, scrawny, short—who were attracting sexy women. The first time I saw a "regular" guy getting rock-star results, I almost rubbed my eyes and questioned reality. Owen Cook was an old-school pickup artist whom I'd read about in *The Game*. (He's left behind pickup artistry to focus solely on self-development.) A five-foot-eight, balding fellow-ginger, he's hardly male-model material. But he understands that attraction is about giving women good emotions, not about a guy's looks. Early in my dating education, I took his boot camp in San Diego. At one club, I watched Cook make out with three different women he had just met—all of them SoCal stunners, all in under ninety minutes. While nowhere near his level at the time, I landed a fistful of phone numbers that weekend, as well as my first instant make-out, which is when you boldly walk up to a woman and, if you read the signals, start kissing in seconds. That weekend taught me that it's not about looks.

But as men, we get hung up on this myth for a couple reasons. First, it's societal conditioning. We're told that good looks are paramount in dating. Also, we tend to value physical beauty in women more than women value it in us. Why? Men are very visual—we love a pretty face and an attractive figure. There's also the ego factor. Nothing puffs out your chest like hearing an envious buddy say, "Dude, your girlfriend's hot!" Because men prioritize looks, we project our preferences onto the opposite sex and assume that women see us the same way. If you'd love to date a model-caliber woman, you might assume that those women want runway-ready guys.

Now, the typical woman would be happy to have a handsome man in her life, sure—but looks are way down on her "must" list. In the poll I mentioned in the last chapter, 64,000 women were asked what traits they want most in a male partner, and physical attractiveness didn't even crack the top ten.

YOUR MOVE: Play to Your Strengths

Focusing on what you think you lack will only hurt your confidence. Play to your strengths, such as your intelligence, wit, or sense of humor. If you make a woman laugh in a flirtatious way (which I'll teach you how to do in Chapter 5), she'll find you as sexy as Brad Pitt, even if you look more like Brad Garrett. My client Jeremy (Higher Self name: "Sexy Beast") had been dateless for two years before he hired me. A restaurant worker who loves Will Ferrell movies, Jeremy is no pretty boy, as he readily admits. "I look like John C. Reilly's uglier brother," he told me during our first meeting. His focus on looks blinded him to his witty, weird sense of humor, which, when he harnessed it, changed his love life. He realized he could simply approach, crack a few jokes, and girls started to dig him. One day he sent me this email:

Connell, my mind is blown! At lunch today, I approached a pro-football cheerleader. I just chatted her up at the salad bar. Had her laughing and loving me. Phone number . . . from a cheer-babe! I feel incredible.

Looks only matter if you let them.

MYTH: Women Want Rich Guys
TRUTH: Women Want Men with Purpose

Back to Jason, my business card–wielding client. That same night on the rooftop in Hollywood, he met a beguiling entertainment attorney. Rather than boasting to her about his high-paying job, he shared how fulfilling it feels when he reshapes an insecure patient's crooked nose or grafts healthy skin onto a burn victim's neck. "I love helping people feel better about their looks," he told her.

Jason led with his heart, not his bank account, and the two of them hit it off.

YOUR MOVE: Express, Don't Impress

I don't care if you're as rich as Scrooge McDuck. Boasting about your financial status will hurt you, not help you, when it comes to women. They want a man of substance, not a man who flashes his fancy creds.

So express, don't impress. Convey the passion you have for the work that's brought you success. Share with women what you love most about your career, how it makes you feel, whom it lets you help.

If you're not a well-to-do guy, no sweat. Women are drawn to men of passion and purpose. Talk about your career ambition, or what excites you about your job. Passion and purpose are cooler than the fastest sports car.

MYTH: Short Guys Struggle with Dating
TRUTH: Women Like Guys of All Shapes and Sizes

Dating is about connection and giving your best, truest self to another person. Do those things and you can have an abundance of romantic options and land a great girlfriend, whether you're six-foot-four or four-foot-six.

Women don't necessarily want tall guys. They want guys who aren't shorter than them. The average American woman is five-foot-four, so if you hit that spot or above on the tape measure, you have lots of options.

And you can also attract girls who are taller than you. For a woman, it's not really about a guy's height. It's about how a guy's height makes her *feel*: namely feminine, smaller, safe. A shorter man can give her those same feelings by adding muscle at the gym, carrying himself with confidence, using his voice in a dominant way, or getting great at flirting.

YOUR MOVE: Feature What You Can't Fix

In business, there's a marketing concept that says, "What you can't fix, you feature." By highlighting a product's weakness, you turn it into a strength. In golf, a nine-holer isn't a lesser course; it's an "executive track." A car isn't too expensive; it's a "luxury automobile." If you're shorter than average, you can joke about it, turning it into a signifier of confidence.

I once went out for the night and found myself wingmanning with a cool, five-foot-four guy named Darren. He was phenomenal with women. Not only did he not care about his height; with several girls he met, he led with it. He told one woman, "When we get married, I can be on the wedding cake," and she laughed so hard, she spit out her drink. To another: "I promise, I'll never look down on you."

So feature what you can't fix. It tells people that you're secure in who you are. And that kind of confidence is sexy to women of all heights.

MYTH: Women Like Bad Boys, Not Nice Guys
TRUTH: Nice Guys Are Sexier Than Six-Pack Abs

From Russell Brand to Jason Statham to Han Solo, many women love the bad boy (and his cousin, the cocky jerk.) The swagger. The bravado. The *Millennium Falcon*. It's irresistible.

Bad boys get girls giggling, twirling their hair, and giving out their numbers. But the odds of women swooning over you—a nice guy—are slim, right?

Wrong. The truth is, you can steal a little bad-boy mojo while still being the nice guy you are. And without getting stuck in the friend zone.

I know this because I'm a nice guy who was raised by nice parents in a nice Ohio town. I volunteer at a residence for blind people. I say please and thank you. I literally help old ladies cross the street. I'm not bragging. Just pointing out that you can be a nice guy and also be *great* with women.

Women are dying to date nice guys. Consider: In a *Glamour* magazine poll, single women chose "loyal and lovable" men as the category of guys they most want to date, at 33 percent. You know who finished second to last, at 6 percent? "Bad boys."[2]

I tried playing the cocky bad boy with women, and I struggled. Then one evening I met a gorgeous, glossy-haired *Maxim* model who opened my eyes to what women are looking for. She was bemoaning all the narcissistic jerks she meets. "I'm so sick of arrogant, selfish men," she said. "I'd love to meet a nice guy, but they never approach me. They're intimidated. It's too bad because nice guys are sexier than six-pack abs—as long as they have a backbone."

Did you catch that? *As long as they have a backbone.* When nice guys strike out with women, it's not because of the niceness. It's because they don't convey the strength and confidence that women respond to.

You don't need to wear some assholier-than-thou mask, and you don't need to be an "alpha male." (More on that in a bit.) You need to be a nice guy with steely self-confidence.

Don't only take my male word on this. "By the time they reach their late twenties, women are done with bad boys," Cherlyn Chong, a relationship coach for women, told me. "They put up with dick pics, arrogance, even emotional abuse, and they just want a nice, honest guy with some form of sexy going on. A guy who's genuine dismantles women's walls by being respectful while unapologetically real. That's sexy as fuck."

YOUR MOVE: Be a Man with a Plan

Women love a leader. When it comes to dates, never say, "So what do *you* wanna do?" Have a plan. Lead. Pick a place she'll love for that first drink and have a second spot in mind for a nightcap. Know where you're taking her, with decisiveness. ("Hey, let's go to [cool place]. It's awesome and you're gonna love it.")

Be a man with a plan, and you can date like a bad boy while being a good guy.

MYTH: It's Creepy to Approach
TRUTH: It's Creepy *Not* to Approach

When I started learning how to attract women, I was at a trendy hotel lounge in New York City one night. My wingman challenged me to approach a table where a cute brunette and her blond friend sat with a muscular guy.

At that point, I was still nervous about talking to women, let alone dealing with a potentially pissed-off boyfriend. And this guy was huge, like a bottle of Muscle Milk made corporeal. But I summoned the courage, walked over, grabbed an empty chair, and offered a warm hello.

The brunette's eyes widened and she leaned forward. "Oh my God! You came right up and talked to us. Do you know what you are?" I thought, *Umm, a creep who's about to get his butt kicked?* "You're *normal!*" She tilted her head toward a fellow sitting a couple tables away. "That guy's been staring at us all night, and it's *creeping us out.*" Oh, and the hulking dude I was worried about? Super friendly. I traded numbers with the brunette, who was as charming as she was pretty.

Most men don't approach women, often from a fear of appearing creepy. But there's nothing creepy about approaching. What feels creepy to women is when a guy wants to approach, yet does nothing except stare.

YOUR MOVE: Follow the Three-Second Rule

When you're in a social environment and you see a woman you'd love to meet, approach her immediately. Begin walking toward her within three seconds of spotting her. If you delay for too long, your Lower Self will talk you out of it, filling you with doubt. The longer you wait, the heavier the weight. Three, two, one . . . go!

MYTH: Women Put Men in the Friend Zone
TRUTH: We Do It to Ourselves

Women don't put us in the friend zone. As men, we do it to ourselves by treating women like platonic pals.

YOUR MOVE: Pull Her Pigtails

A lot of women enjoy it when a guy teases her. It's a playful way of saying *I like you.* Think Cary Grant in classic rom-coms such as *Bringing Up Baby.* Grant and his love interest Katharine Hepburn are mistakenly thrown in jail. "When they find out who we are, they'll let us out," she says. "When they find out who *you* are, they'll pad the cell," he replies. Girls tend to like it when you pull their proverbial pigtails.

The trick? Tease her for silly, trivial things—nothing she would actually take personally—say, if she's ten minutes late for your date, or if her favorite movie is *Legally Blonde.*

It's not about "negging" her, as some pickup artists teach. It's an invitation to flirt. Teasing invites your date to spar with you, and banter can send chemistry soaring.

MYTH: Your Conversational Skills Must Be Amazing
TRUTH: You Can Lower the Conversational Bar

You don't need to be the wittiest guy on the block to get a woman into you. In fact, trying to "up your game" and straining to be clever and charismatic can create tension and make you come across as try-hard and inauthentic.

YOUR MOVE: Be Borderline Boring

Remember: You're talking to a girl, not giving a TED Talk or doing a stand-up comedy set. Lower the bar for how good your word choice needs to be. Paradoxically, this will improve the conversational flow, since by relaxing you allow your naturally clever and charismatic side to arise.

MYTH: Sex Equals Happiness
TRUTH: Fulfillment Comes from Growing and Giving

A guy I know has hooked up with more than four hundred women, and he's still miserable. For him, sex is not a form of deep connection or love. It's ego candy and temporary physical satisfaction. After a new "lay," as he calls them, he briefly feels attractive, special—but the feeling vanishes fast.

In his excellent book *The Mask of Masculinity*, Lewis Howes, a former professional football player, writes that for many single men, "life has become a never-ending trophy hunt, but none of them end up actually feeling like a winner . . . It's not about intimacy—it's about arithmetic. And yet the math always turns out to be disappointing."[3]

It's fine to sow a wild oat or two. But continuously sleeping around is a dead-end path: It might boost your confidence short-term, but it won't fulfill you long-term.

YOUR MOVE: Make Your Love Life About Growing and Giving

For true dating fulfillment, you must grow and you must give. Grow into a more authentic version of you and give to a wonderful woman from your soul's depths.

MYTH: Women Love Alpha Males
TRUTH: Alpha Males Aren't a Thing[4]

In a BO-drenched Las Vegas conference room, a strutting pickup coach was onstage praising the supposed panty-dropping powers of being a dominant man. "The alpha male gets all the tail," he said with Johnnie Cochran flair.

But there's a problem here: Alpha males aren't a thing.

The idea of the alpha male first gained credence in the 1970s when wildlife biologist L. David Mech, an expert in wolves, published a book that documented the existence of alpha wolves in the wild. Two decades later, he tried to replicate his findings, but he couldn't. He was horrified. It turns out, the "alpha" behavior he thought he'd observed was simply mom and dad wolves caring for their pups. Mech renounced his original findings, but it was too late; the myth of the alpha had cemented into conventional wisdom.

It's also informed a lot of bad dating advice. There's no concrete, scientific evidence for so-called alpha males getting to mate with all the females—in any animals, including humans. Take our closest relatives the chimpanzees. Studies show that the aggressive chimp doesn't necessarily become the group leader, and that smaller, more docile chimps become dominant by completing more feminine tasks, such as grooming other chimps. And our other closest biological relatives are bonobos, apes that live in a matriarchal society. (Humans and bonobos are the only species that French-kiss, a fun fact that could get you some right-swipes from animal lovers if you include it on your Tinder profile.)

Traits like assertiveness, courage, and boldness are absolutely essential in dating. A woman must sense your strength. But the idea of the alpha male is a myth and a troublesome one. At worst, alpha-male behavior stifles growth and encourages men to view women and "beta males" as inferior. At best, it leads to wearing Axe body spray, chest bumps, and saying things like brah and baller.

YOUR MOVE: Drop the "Alpha" Mask

It just doesn't work. Yes, there are times when you must take decisive action, "man up," and make a move. But studies show that non-alpha qualities like kindness and generosity are the key indicators of fulfilling relationships.

MYTH: Rejection Sucks
TRUTH: Rejection Is Necessary—and Can Be Good for You!

This is the biggest, baddest myth of all because it causes so many problems.

Dating sucks because rejection sucks. You take a chance with your heart—you ask a girl out, you send that flirty text—and if you get turned down, you feel wounded.

But what causes the pain is not rejection itself. It's how you interpret it. You give it a painful meaning. You turn it into evidence that you're not attractive to the kinds of women you want to date.

You see, all men (and all people in general, really) want to feel special and important. This driving force is hardwired into our psyche. It's why we climb mountains or pump iron. Hell, I wrote this book in part so I can tell the world, "I'm an author, bitches!" It makes me feel cooler.

One of the most powerful ways to feel special and important is through dating. Validation from the right woman can be intoxicating. It helps you realize something powerful: You are enough. And there's nothing wrong with this.

But when you get rejected, it can make you doubt your romantic worth. You feel less special, misinterpreting that rejection as a sign that you're unattractive. Then you extrapolate: If you're not attractive to women, if you're not enough, then maybe you won't get to give or receive love, and that would lead either to loneliness or to settling—both awful outcomes. That's heavy stuff.

Viewing rejection through this lens turns any romantic risk into Judgment Day for your worth as a man. So you probably don't take risks and pursue the kinds of girls you're drawn to, because rejection would cut deep, making you feel unattractive and less of a man. And if you do take a chance and, say, approach a woman you find attractive, you likely can't relax and be your best self, which leads to *more* rejection. It's a vicious downward spiral.

YOUR MOVE: See Rejection Through New Eyes

When I take a client out for in-person wingman training, I want him to see me get rejected. I have him choose a scary approach situation—say, a large group of girls on the dance floor—and I go in, talking to the cutest one. I often (but not always) get rebuffed. I do this not because I'm a masochist. My client needs to see rejection not as something to fear but as part of the dating process. It's required. You can't approach women and *not* get turned down from time to time. You can't get Tinder matches and *not* get ghosted occasionally. It's part of putting yourself out there.

What if you saw rejection as painless? What if you were immune? What if you gave far fewer fucks? You could take new, bold actions and with lots of confidence.

I want you to see rejection for what it is: no biggie. A woman's rejection is not—I repeat, *not*—evidence of your worth or importance. It's merely evidence that she's not interested. Maybe you're very attractive but just not her type.

Rejection means next to nothing. You can brush it off, just as you do when the restaurant hostess "rejects" your request for a brunch table on a busy Sunday, or when the Delta ticket agent "rejects" your request for a business-class upgrade. Look at dating rejection the same way. Your worth isn't on the line. It's not personal.

Now, you might be saying, "You're nuts! Of course it's personal. It's my love life!" To which I reply, "Why are you talking to a book? It can't hear you."

The truth is, a woman who barely knows you can't truly reject you. Now, if your long-term girlfriend says, "I don't love you, you've never made me orgasm, and I'm leaving you for Fabio," okay, now *that* is rejection. But if a woman you barely know blows you off, she may simply be saying she likes the Beatles, and you're the Stones. No shame there. The Stones fucking rock.

Much of this book is about creating a model for your love life in which there is no rejection. When you realize that it doesn't even exist, then there's nothing to fear—and you can achieve great things.

But we're getting ahead of ourselves. For now, just know that not only is rejection not all that bad—it's an essential part of the process.

Turn the page to build a bulletproof mind and take your dating life to a new level.

SO WHAT HAVE WE LEARNED?
....

- Buying into myths such as "Your Looks Matter" can hurt your love life, leading to either poor actions or to inaction.
- Rejection is just information, not a personal indictment of your worth. A woman who barely knows you can't truly reject you. It's time to give far fewer fucks about it.
- Despite all his money, Scrooge McDuck doesn't wear pants. The rich really aren't like the rest of us.
- Tattoo this on the body part of your choice: *You are enough.*

YOUR SUCKY LOVE LIFE IS YOUR FAULT
(AND THAT'S A GOOD THING)

BUILDING CORE CONFIDENCE

> Nine-tenths of the ills from which intelligent people
> suffer spring from their intellect.
> —Marcel Proust, *Within a Budding Grove*; French novelist[1]

> I'm trying to think but nothin' happens.
> —Curly Howard, *Calling All Curs*; American Stooge[2]

. . . .

Let's start with a little thought experiment, in two scenarios.

1. You're in your favorite coffee shop, and you see an attractive woman. Your only goal? Walk over and ask her for the time. As you go up to her, how comfortable and confident would you feel on a scale of 1 to 10?

2. Same coffee shop, same woman. Except now your mission is different: "Approach" her, use a clever opener, be charismatic, spark attraction, and get her digits for a date. If this is your goal, using that same 1 to 10 scale, what's your confidence level?

Odds are, when you compare the two numbers, in the first scenario your confidence lands in the 7 to 10 range, while in the second it nosedives to about 1 to 4. ("Put me down for minus-100," one client told me when we walked through this exercise.)

Now, both situations involve identical actions: You walk up to an attractive female stranger and start talking. But one context gives you confidence, and the other makes you anxious, perhaps even petrified.

Why the disparity? It's all in your mind—specifically, the stories you tell yourself based on your beliefs. You likely imbue the two situations with very different meanings. Asking a stranger for the time carries no risk to your ego. Your self-worth is not on the line. But "hitting on her" has much higher stakes. In this story, success means that you'll feel attractive and land a date with a beauty who might be The One. Yet if you approach and fail, you may feel humiliated, rejected, creepy, and learn that the worst is true: Women just aren't into you. May as well give up on finding a regular girlfriend and settle for the inflatable kind.

This second interpretation—*Failure means I'm not enough*—triggers fear and anxiety. It turns talking to a woman into an existential reckoning on your worth as a man.

It's these misperceptions about yourself that govern your actions and emotions and determine your dating destiny.

I'm here to help you change that voice in your head. In this chapter, you'll learn how to build bulletproof confidence, so that anxiety-inducing actions like approaching or moving in for the first kiss become almost as easy as asking for the time. You'll also learn the Five Beliefs That Ensure Success, while destroying the limiting thought that most holds you back. And you'll craft a clear, compelling vision for your love life that will excite and motivate you.

Now, you may be yearning to skip ahead to the chapters on techniques, moves, and lines. But hang with me, because the right mindset is 80 percent of dating success. It's what summons your confident, authentic Higher Self every day. It's what makes the moves and lines work.

LOOK IN "THE MIRROR"

In my twenties, I worked as a waiter at a steak house. I had a huge crush on Tina, a smart, sassy, doe-eyed waitress. One night, I was leaning against the break room wall and sucking on a cherry lollipop when Tina walked up to me, pulled the sucker from my mouth, and slowly put it in hers. "Yum," she cooed, holding eye contact.

Every atom in my body was aroused, but despite her bold, flirtatious move, it never occurred to me that she liked me, so I didn't ask her out or flirt back. I was *certain* that I wasn't attractive to women, so I figured she just wanted my lollipop. I had no idea she "wanted my lollipop."

A limiting perception about your attractiveness can blind you to opportunities and stop you from taking the actions that create connections with women.

This leads me to some bad news and some good news.

The bad news: If things aren't working in your romantic life, it's on you. Everything you love, hate, feel, fear, think, believe—it all shows up in your interactions with women, for better or worse. Your dating life is a mirror that reflects what's happening inside your head. It comes through in your voice, words, eye contact, actions, emotions. Take Tina and me, for example. It wasn't that I was afraid to ask her out; instead, it was that asking her out never entered my mind because I was sure that women didn't want me.

The quality of your love life correlates to the quality of your mindset.

Saying that your dating struggles are your fault may sound harsh, but it's actually excellent news! You can't change external factors—women, society, Tinder's algorithm. But you can change your mindset, which will change your emotions, actions, and outcomes.

To be clear, there's nothing broken in you. You don't need fixing. But you do need to fix your mindset.

Before we go further, here's a simple rule I want you to follow in your dating life: Take full responsibility for your results. If you don't, you can start to see yourself as a victim. Too many men make excuses for their dating woes, blaming external forces. Never see yourself as a victim. It can foster resentment toward women, which makes you less attractive. And it robs you of the agency to change things. Beware of buying into a victim mentality. When something isn't working in your dating life, take responsibility for fixing it. Take total ownership.

THE POWER OF BELIEFS
....

What's a belief? It's a feeling of absolute certainty about what something means. In other words, it's a story you repeatedly tell yourself to the point that you hold it as incontrovertible fact. Many beliefs are true (*Mom loves me; Hard work pays off*), while others are false but fairly harmless (*I'll have one more cookie; That Bruce Willis can really act!*).

Then there are limiting beliefs—disempowering feelings that are either totally or partially false but that constrain you, damaging the quality of your life. In dating, limiting beliefs can keep you from taking the right action and also hurt your results when you do. And they can crush your confidence.

For example, a guy might think, *I'm not good-looking enough to date beautiful women*, even though he's never even tried. Therefore, he doesn't pursue the women he's attracted to, effectively turning a made-up story into a self-fulfilling prophecy.

Here are some common limiting beliefs:

- I'm not good-looking/cool/tall enough to date attractive women.
- I don't have the words/don't know what to say to girls.
- I'm the wrong ethnicity.
- I'm not outgoing enough/I'm too shy and introverted.
- I'm too old.

When you replace a limiting belief with a new, empowering, and *true* one, it changes how you feel, makes dating more fun, and propels you toward what I call an Amazing Outcome—a dating life full of confidence and connection.

"Whether you believe something is true or you believe it's not, you're right," motivational speaker Tony Robbins contends in his *Unlimited Power* audio coaching program. "Your beliefs literally open up the floodgate that opens up your power and possibility. Limiting beliefs shut you down and chain you to limitation. If you want the key, you have to adopt a new belief."[3]

The most destructive, disempowering dating belief? It's some version of *I'm not enough.* That you're not tall enough or handsome enough or charismatic enough for the kind of woman you want to date. And getting so-called proof that you're not enough—a woman ghosts you or friend-zones you or turns down your approach—can make you feel like less of a man.

But when you destroy the attitudes that hold you back, you're free to take new actions—even if those limitations seem, well, truly limiting.

A decade ago, I was in London on a sunny Sunday afternoon, attending a dating boot camp as a student. As part of an assignment, I'd spent two hours approaching women in Trafalgar Square. At the time, I was still battling the doubts that triggered anxiety: *What if I'm not good-looking enough? What if I'm too introverted?* In other words, *What if I'm not enough?* My coach was offering some pointers when he spotted a past client of his in mid-approach. "There's Aaron," my coach said. "Looks like he's doing great." I turned to see a guy chatting with a tall, slender brunette woman wearing aviator shades and a formfitting trench coat. Aaron looked utterly relaxed. At one point, the woman laughed and threw her hair back. She was clearly loving him. It didn't matter to her that Aaron was in a wheelchair. He was all smiles and smoothness, bound to his chair but not to his limitations.

THE FIVE BELIEFS THAT ENSURE SUCCESS

....

I want to share five beliefs that, if applied, will make great dating results a veritable lock for you. You could stop reading after this chapter and still transform the quality of your love life, by following these North Stars. Here they are.

1. **You Are Enough:** When I was a junior in college, I wrote a weekly humor column for the campus newspaper. It was a popular feature, but I was painfully insecure about my writing. One day, a fan letter from a journalism professor appeared in my mailbox. "You may not know how good you are," the professor said of my writing, before telling me about the promising career that awaited me. That let-

ter, that sentence, was the booster shot of confidence that I badly needed.

You may not know how good *you* are. If you wonder whether or not you're good enough to date wonderful women and get a great girlfriend, you absolutely are—in ways big and small. Buy into this. Because when you believe it, everything shifts. (At the end of the chapter, I'll give you an exercise to help you better appreciate what a great catch you are.)

You can't truly connect with a woman until you connect with your own awesomeness.

2. **When You Focus on an Amazing Outcome, Your Mind Makes It Happen:** Accept the truth that a smart, sweet, sexy woman *will* be in your life. It's a done deal—it's just a matter of *when*, not *if*. It is about focusing on what you want, rather than what you fear. Anxiety and inaction come from playing a horror movie in your mind. So play a different flick, one that shows you a compelling outcome.

I'm not talking about a ruthless fixation on success. Don't go all *Whiplash* on yourself. Simply soak in the certitude that an incredible love life awaits. It will happen.

This is not woo-woo, Law of Attraction mumbo jumbo. It's practical psychology. When you commit to a compelling goal, your subconscious says, "Let's do this!" And to keep you honest, your brain does a dickishly cool thing by making you stressed out if your actions don't align with your goal. To avoid this pain, you act in accordance with your desires, and your mind deletes many of the shitty thoughts and behaviors that hold you back.

Also, this kind of fierce focus helps you perform at a higher level. It's what great athletes do. In his prime, on his way to winning fifteen majors, Tiger Woods would stand on the tee and picture the blade of grass on which his ball would land some 350 yards away. By focusing on where he was going, he worried less about sand traps and lakes. This relaxed him, facilitating his best play.

If you don't envision your ideal dating life, you'll never have one. See and feel your outcome—the confidence, the romantic connection—and your inner self will find a way to make it happen.

3. **Rituals Equal Results:** Love handles or washboard abs? Being dead broke or Richie Rich wealthy? Unlucky in love or honeymooning in Hawaii? Our progress in any area, or lack thereof, comes from our rituals, the actions we take consistently. Committing to daily action will propel you toward the romantic fulfillment you desire.

You can visualize and meditate and get your kumbayas out all day long, but if you don't take consistent, ritualized action, your chance of failure is high. Vision boards and goals scribbled on paper are just dead wood without the discipline to act.

But don't think you need to improve in leaps and bounds right away. Yes, big breakthroughs happen, but don't underestimate the power of steady, incremental improvement. "The difference a tiny improvement can make over time is astounding," James Clear writes in his book *Atomic Habits*, adding, "[I]f you can get 1 percent better each day for one year, you'll end up thirty-seven times better by the time you're done."[4]

At the end of this chapter, I'll teach you the Confidence Kickoff—a morning ritual that ensures you spend every day in an empowering, action-taking mindset, with your Higher Self running the show. Becoming the man you want to be demands consistent effort. It's a New Year's resolution that you make 365 days a year.

4. **Fear Is Your Friend, Not Your Foe:** With apologies to FDR, the only thing we have to fear is ignoring fear itself. Fear can be a friend, a powerful force to harness, a call to action.

If you're afraid to approach that girl or go for the first-date kiss, that's fear telling you exactly what you *should* do. Your love life is like a boat, and fear is the wind. You can use those gusts to reach your destination or do nothing and be lost at sea. As Tony Robbins said at a seminar, "You can't control the wind, but you can control the sails."

Commit, right now, to doing one scary but necessary thing every day. Yes, this means leaving your comfort zone. That's the price. You have a choice: comfort now, pain later. Or pain now, comfort later.

Let your fear guide you, and you'll see incredible results faster than you thought possible.

5. **Failure Is the Secret to Results:** Thomas Edison failed to invent the light bulb hundreds of times. Abraham Lincoln failed to win almost every election he entered, until 1860. J. K. Rowling's first *Harry Potter* manuscript was rejected by twelve publishing houses.

So-called failure is just part of the path to achievement. So don't be afraid to fail big and to fail often. Then fail again and again and again . . . Until you succeed.

HOW TO TRANSFORM
A LIMITING BELIEF
....

I want to show you exactly how to take any bummer of a belief and replace it with a new, empowering one that will give you much more confidence with women. You'll do this exercise at the end of the chapter. For now, follow along as my client Robert (Higher Self name: "Rocket Rob") uses my eight-step process to destroy and replace his biggest bullshit belief.

MEET "ROCKET ROB"
Robert, fifty-one, is an accountant and father of three. On the day I met him, he was emerging from a rough divorce, which ended twenty-plus years of marriage. He wanted to go out and meet women but, as he told me, "Who'd want to date an old, divorced dad like me?"

Two nights later, at a tropical-themed lounge, Robert boldly walked up to Sofia, a smart, funny, thirty-one-year-old HR rep in a red dress. Within twenty minutes, they were making out and setting up a date.

How did he do it? By changing his beliefs, starting with simply answering these questions. Read them, then do yourself a favor and answer them for yourself.

Q: What belief about yourself most holds you back with women? What "story" hurts your dating confidence?

WHAT ROBERT SAID: "That I can't attract and keep a high-quality woman because I'm too old and not handsome enough."

COACH'S TAKE: Robert felt old and unattractive—despite the fact that lots of women date older guys, and that he's a good-looking man with wavy salt-and-pepper hair.

YOUR TURN: What story do you tell yourself that most hurts your confidence?

Q: What's the "payoff" of this belief? What does it do for you, or allow you *not* to do?

WHAT ROBERT SAID: "This belief gives me an excuse not to approach. I can stay comfortable. I'll never get dumped or rejected. I don't have to go to the gym because I have no one to impress."

COACH'S TAKE: A bad belief earns its keep, in an insidious way. It gives you something. Usually, it helps you avoid short-term pain or discomfort—but that comes with a long-term cost.

YOUR TURN: How does your limiting belief pay off for you? Does it keep you from asking out your crush and getting turned down? Does it shield you from rejection?

Q: How do you feel about yourself when you fully buy into this belief?

WHAT ROBERT SAID: "I feel old, unattractive, like shit. A beta male. I just feel small and unworthy, and alone—without dating options. It saps my motivation. I feel sad and stuck."

COACH'S TAKE: By attaching pain to your belief, you begin to feel the consequences of having this parasite squirming around in your head.

YOUR TURN: How do you feel when your belief is running the show? Small? A failure? Less of a man? Truthfully answering this question will sting, but it's important.

Q: What price have you paid for this belief? What price *will* you pay five years from now if this belief continues weighing you down? What has it, and will it, cost you?

WHAT ROBERT SAID: "My belief has cost me confidence. My work has suffered. God, think of all the women I could have dated! I've been lonely a lot of nights. It's cost me intimacy, connection, sex, love. In five years, I'll be drinking more, and I'll probably settle again for a wife I'm not that into—and that means another divorce. Depressing."

COACH'S TAKE: You pay a steep price for your limiting beliefs. Getting clear on the consequences of holding on to them—past, present, and future—can motivate you to change.

YOUR TURN: Write out the heftiest prices you've paid. What has your belief cost you? What is it costing you now? What will life look like five years from now if your dating life is exactly the same?

Q: Be a detective. What might be untrue about your limiting belief? How might this story be bullshit?

WHAT ROBERT SAID: "Women have told me I'm handsome. I have a couple friends my age who date attractive women. If they can do it, maybe I can!"

COACH'S TAKE: Like a cop interrogating a witness, poke holes in your old story. Just a little doubt is all you need to make your old belief start to crumble.

YOUR TURN: Look for any evidence that your limiting belief is fiction, or perhaps only partially true. Example: You think you're too short to date tall women, but you've seen guys your height or shorter with women much taller than them.

Q: If this limiting belief vanished, what actions would you take? How would you feel about yourself? What could you achieve?

WHAT ROBERT SAID: "I could get a smart, sexy, younger girlfriend. I could approach and be confident. I'd be more motivated to hit the gym. I'd feel like a new man. And the future would look incredible. Just blue skies."

COACH'S TAKE: When a limiting belief disappears, it's like a curse has lifted. You feel lighter, freer—like great things are possible.

YOUR TURN: Paint a vivid picture of the kinds of women you'd date and the way you would feel if you were free from your limiting belief.

Q: What *new* belief would propel you to your Amazing Outcome?

WHAT ROBERT SAID: "My new belief: 'I am irresistible to many bright, beautiful women of all ages because I'm successful, handsome, and big-hearted.'"

COACH'S TAKE: His new belief is fantastic—the total opposite of his old one. It's also true. After writing this new belief, Robert was excited to go meet women.

YOUR TURN: Write a new belief that would propel you toward your own Amazing Outcome. A tip: Begin your new belief with the words "I am . . ." This ties your belief to your identity, making it more powerful. And it helps to support this statement with specifics. For example, "I am attractive to many women because I'm kind, smart, successful, and can make them laugh."

Q: What evidence supports your new belief?

WHAT ROBERT SAID: "Quite a few women have said I'm handsome or showed interest. The cute girl behind the check-in counter at my gym always says, 'Hi, handsome,' when I show my ID. And I know I have a big heart."

COACH'S TAKE: For a belief to feel real, you need evidence to support it. Try to find some from your past or present. If your new belief is, "I am charismatic enough to attract a pretty girlfriend," think back to moments when you felt charismatic or times when women showed interest in you. The most powerful evidence of all? With this book as your guide, get *new* experiences that confirm your new belief, as Robert did when he went out and met Sofia.

YOUR TURN: Go get new evidence! Your mind needs proof that your new belief is true. And it's okay if you don't fully buy into your new belief right away. It takes time, but with new experiences, you'll realize that this *new* you is the *real* you.

CHAPTER 3 MISSIONS

....

Four Steps to Building Core Confidence:

1. **Define Your Amazing Dating Outcome**

   You need a clear, compelling vision for your dating life that gets you excited, juiced. It's your Amazing Outcome. When you lack this compelling vision, you lack direction and motivation. This is the problem with New Year's resolutions, which have an 80 percent failure rate. (Most people quit by mid-February.)[5]

   But when you know exactly what your outcome is, even when you get off- track, you know your destination and can correct course. When a jet takes off from JFK for a coast-to-coast flight, it strays from its intended flight path much of the time, as the pilot adjusts for turbulence and other planes. But it lands at LAX right on the white stripe.

   Your Amazing Outcome should have three elements.

   - It's amazing to *you*. It excites and juices you.
   - It's measurable (examples: "two dates weekly"; "get a sweet girlfriend I love by the holidays").
   - It's an outcome—a place of arrival.

   To turbocharge your Amazing Outcome, know your *why*—the deeper reasons you want to achieve it. What will your outcome let you feel or give? How will you grow? A strong *why* gets you in touch with your deeper purpose, fueling you to massive action. (At the same time, understand that life-changing results will take time. Your love life is like an ocean liner—there's a lag between turning the captain's wheel and changing course.)

   Here's an example of an Amazing Outcome from my client Brad: "To overcome approach anxiety so that I can meet women at night in the bars and also in the daytime. I would like to date around for a while and then choose a great girlfriend based on who I connect with the most. I would like to be in a relationship in six months or less." His *why*: "It's about feeling more confident and attractive, knowing I didn't settle. Also, I love being a boyfriend and having that companionship."

2. **List Twenty-Five Awesome Traits You Offer Women**
If you're like most men, you tend to focus on what you think you lack, rather than what you offer. Instead, let's focus on some of the specific reasons why you're a great choice for women. This shift of focus will boost your confidence.

List twenty-five reasons why you're an awesome catch. Don't overthink this. Underthink it! There's no wrong answer, as long as each item is specific.

A sample from my Awesome List: "1) I like and respect women . . . 7) I'm a good kisser . . . 12) I know every Beatles song by heart . . . 17) I make great French toast . . . 22) I wrote a flipping book!" This is from my client Derrick: "3) I have a modern vehicle for transportation . . . 12) I graduated with a BA in criminal justice . . . 18) I'm taking care of my aging parents . . . 23) I'm a thrifty man."

If you like, don't stop at twenty-five. If you dig deep, you can find 125 reasons why you're an awesome choice for any woman. So get to brainstorming.

3. **Identify, Destroy, and Replace Your Biggest Limiting Belief**
Following the same eight-question process I used with Robert, replace the biggest limiting belief you have about women with a new, empowering belief that will propel you toward your Amazing Outcome.

4. **Complete a Daily "Confidence Kickoff"**
To reach your Amazing Outcome, you *must* put yourself in a powerful, confident emotional state, and you *must* do it virtually every day. If you're not in a great state, your Lower Self

will take the wheel and drive your dating life into oncoming traffic. We don't want that.

To make sure your Higher Self stays in charge, do a daily Confidence Kickoff—a fifteen-minute (minimum) morning session that summons your best, most authentic self. This will set your emotional thermostat at the right level, making it much easier for you to take action, plow through challenges, and do the missions I'll be giving you.

Every morning, find a quiet place and for at least fifteen minutes, do the following three steps. (If it helps, divide these into three five-minute chunks. And feel free to listen to music that centers your mind.)

Focus on Gratitude: What are you deeply grateful for? Recall specific moments that were filled with love, joy, sexiness, wonder—anything positive. My go-to memory? My dad's surprise eighty-fifth birthday party, which I planned with my three sisters. It was extra special because my mom, who was very sick and didn't have much time left, held on long enough to be there. It was the best day of my life.

What moments make you deeply grateful? Flood your mind with vivid thoughts or images. It's almost impossible to simultaneously feel gratitude and stress.

Recite Your New Belief: Say your new belief out loud five times, and do it with positive, excited emotion. For example, you might say, "I am *devastatingly* sexy to many women because I'm smart, well-traveled, and a great kisser." I repeat: Say it OUT LOUD. No cheating. This may sound silly, but verbalizing it with emotion helps embed this new belief in your psyche. (Google "inner speech of behavioral regulation" if you want to nerd out on why this works.)

See a "Future Memory": Go into the future and "see" an experience you *will* have after you reach your Amazing Outcome. You can visualize it, verbalize it, or write it down. ("In the future, my girlfriend and I will drive cross-country in my convertible . . .") Maybe your future memory is simply you getting a cute girl's number at the gym or cooking dinner with your soul mate on a Saturday night. Don't edit yourself. It can be G-rated or XXX—as long as it puts a smile on your face. Do this every day during your Confidence Kickoff, and come up with new future memories as you progress.

Make your Confidence Kickoff a daily ritual, okay? It will keep you connected to your Amazing Outcome, which will motivate you to smash through challenges as they arise—and they will.

SO WHAT HAVE WE LEARNED?
....

- Your beliefs determine your dating destiny—for better or worse.
- An Amazing Outcome fuels you to take massive action in your love life.
- Do a Confidence Kickoff every day to set your emotional thermostat and summon your most resourceful self.
- Focus on what you offer, not what you (think) you lack. You can't connect with a woman until you connect with your own awesomeness.
- When a woman puts your lollipop in *her* mouth, yes— that's flirting.
- Remember: You. Are. Enough. After you do mission 2, you'll have twenty-five pieces of proof that this is true.

⚡ BONUS TIP ⚡

HOW TO DESTROY FEAR OF "REJECTION"

Jared, thirty-seven, is a U.S. Navy captain. As the two of us walked into Madison Square Park on a spring day to meet women, the beads of sweat on his forehead betrayed his nervousness. "I've never approached girls before," he said.

He feared (cue: scary music) *rejection*. But he quickly got two phone numbers, one from a cute premed student out walking her dog, the second from a Brazilian tourist lounging on a blanket. Two for two!

Next, I sent Jared over to approach a woman on a bench, her nose in a book. He came back a few minutes later with a huge grin on his face. I assumed he'd grabbed a third number, but it was the opposite.

He'd been rejected. And I'd never seen him happier.

"It was fantastic," he said. "She told me, 'I just want to read my book. Bye.' So I bounced."

"Yet you survived," I said, poking his shoulder. You're still here, in the flesh."

As good as getting two phone numbers felt, his *aha!* moment was realizing that with the right mindset, rejection is no biggie.

"*That's* what I've been so afraid of all these years?" Jared said. "That didn't hurt at all. There's really nothing to fear." And when there's nothing to fear, you become free to approach with confidence.

CHAPTER 4

FOR ADDED VALUE, ADD SOME VALUES

> If you know the enemy and know yourself,
> your victory will not stand in doubt.
> —Sun Tzu, *The Art of War*[1]

> Resistance by definition is self-sabotage.
> —Steven Pressfield, *The War of Art*[2]

....

Not interested." "Leave me alone!" "Fuck off."

The rejections rained down hard and fast that Saturday night in Las Vegas, a year into my quest to transform my love life. I was with a few guy friends at XS, an open-air nightclub on the Strip with a gold-accented dance floor and a sprawling poolside patio. I'd vowed to spend two hours there to work on my approaching skills, but it had been a rough start, and I was gonna call it a night.

On my way out, I hit the men's room, and as I went to wash my hands I glanced up at the mirror and saw a quitter. Giving up after a few tough approaches had become a pattern for me. I'd go out to a lounge or club and, after I endured a rejection or two, I'd bounce.

I looked at my reflection in disgust, asking out loud, "Would LeBron go two for fourteen and leave at halftime? No! You're not quitting, you little bitch! Be. Resilient." The bow-tied bathroom attendant raised an eyebrow.

With a post–pep talk bounce in my step, I hit the bar for a glass of Irish courage. "Jameson neat," I said. I heard a friendly voice from my left: "I ordered the same thing!" I turned to see a bright smile beneath mischievous brunette curls. Her cut-off Bart Simpson tee revealed a sparkly stud on her toned stomach. *Wow.*

She introduced herself, and Nora and I began chatting. When I told her I was a writer, her eyes got wide. We talked about our favorite nonfiction books. (She loved Hunter Thompson's political writing but felt *Hell's Angels* was overrated.) As we discussed her passion for playing bass (she was in a rock band) and her budding modeling career, it was clear that we were hitting it off. I invited her back to my hotel room, a short walk away, to listen to side two of *Abbey Road*. She said sure.

We were sitting on the couch in my suite, but as the album neared its end, I still hadn't made a move. It was fear. *What if she shoots me down?* I thought.

Finally, I found the courage and leaned in for the kiss. She kissed me back. Seconds later she was straddling me, scolding me: "About time. You were almost in the friend zone." We started a months-long fling.

The next day, a friend who'd seen me leave the club with Nora gave me a high five: "Bro, every guy was staring at her," he said. "How'd you do it?"

Simple: I followed the right values.

In this chapter, I'm going to teach you a new set of values that will free you from doubt, fear, and inner conflict, and in doing so, improve all areas of your love life—from approaching to first dates to finding the courage to go for the kiss. You'll also get practical steps you can take today to get momentum that propels you toward your dream girlfriend. And the best part: You'll do all this as the most awesome, confident you.

Upgrading your values is like upgrading your dating software, going from slow, bug-ridden Windows 97 to the latest high-speed operating system. It's time to reboot.

USE THE FORCE
....

You've gotten dating advice before, right? I assume I'm not the first expert who's told you to approach, be bold, ask out your crush. You could close this book right now and find countless online gurus to give you fairly sound technique. You more or less know what to do, but you don't do it. Why?

Because, young Jedi—much conflict in you, there is.

You see, there's an invisible force inside of you that creates doubt and fear, keeping you from taking the actions that will help you reach your dating potential. (More on this force in just a bit.) Yet when you learn to control what's happening inside, you can summon the confidence to take new, better actions and transform your love life.

All you have to do is act in accordance with the right values.

Every romantic success and failure you've had, every action you've taken or not taken, has been guided by your values—even if you're not aware of them.

So what exactly are values? As Tony Robbins explains in many of his programs as well as in his book *Awaken the Giant Within*, they're the feelings, ideas, and emotional states that you place the most importance on. They govern your actions and outcomes in every area of life, and in the area of dating they might include love, sexual connection, growth, adventure, and self-worth, among many others.[3]

When you use a flawed value system, problems arise in your love life. You experience inner conflict, take less action, get fewer dates, and feel less confident.

But with the right values in place . . .

- Conflicts vanish, letting you confidently approach women.
- You become funnier and more charismatic on dates.
- You feel a powerful sense of peace and inner alignment.
- Dating becomes more fun.

The right values are like a compass pointing you toward your desired destination. But the wrong values can throw your compass out of whack. You get lost and wind up in the Bermuda Love Triangle.

Here are some of the values men focus on in their dating lives:

- Love/Connection
- Success/Results
- Freedom
- Safety/Certainty
- Adventure
- Confidence
- Fun/Playful/Humor
- Vulnerability
- Warmth
- Feeling Attractive/Sexy

- Resilience
- Passion/Sexual Desire
- Courage
- Self-Improvement
- Integrity
- Excitement
- Charisma
- Honesty
- Patience
- Gratitude

On the other side of these values is that powerful force I mentioned a bit earlier: Rejection. It's sort of an anti-value. You badly want to avoid it. Feeling rejected is destructive because it can unlock deeper pain—loneliness, anger, unworthiness, inferiority, even depression.

Simply put, Rejection is a big ball of suck.

You, me, every single guy—we're always trying to experience those positive emotional states and at the same time avoid Rejection. It's a survival mechanism that's hardwired into our psyche. Humans seek pleasure and avoid pain. And this is what creates so much inner conflict. Dating that beautiful woman would feel great, but getting rejected would feel bad.

These values guide your focus every day. Different guys prioritize different values, and everyone has their own personal chart-topper—the value you seek above all others. At or near the top of your list might be, say, Success/Results—a great date, an awesome Tinder match. For another guy, Romance may be his thing; he wants to Lady-and-the-Tramp-it at an Italian joint with his dream date. And yet a different dude might value Feeling Attractive/Sexy above all else.

Your top value is a warm bubble bath with your favorite rubber duckie. And Rejection is a vat of acid.

DISCOVER YOUR
"BIG THREE" VALUES
....

It helps to know the values that you prioritize because, as you'll soon see, values that don't serve you can hurt your dating outcomes. To discover your Big Three, ask yourself, *What emotional states or ideas are most important to me in my dating life?*

Knowing your values can bring your inner conflicts into stark relief. Take my client Jeff (Higher Self name: "MVP"), thirty-seven, a U.S. Army veteran who lives on the West Coast. He came to me because he wanted help approaching. I asked him how many attractive women he'd seen in the last six months. "Maybe five hundred," he said. "They're everywhere!" And how many had he talked to? "Zero," he said with embarrassment. "I'm so confident in other areas. I mean, I've been shot at. I can handle life-or-death situations, but I can't walk up to a cute girl."

How could a cool, confident soldier go zero for five hundred when it comes to approaching? Simple: inner conflict. In his case, it was a heavyweight bout of Love vs. Rejection.

Talking with him, I quickly learned that Jeff's top value was Love. More than anything, he just wants to give and receive it. Beautiful! But Rejection can trigger painful emotions. Jeff said the thought of being shot down would make him feel ugly, less worthy of love.

On one hand, he wanted to approach and find a great girl to love. On the other, he feared that Rejection would make him feel unlovable. No wonder Jeff couldn't approach.

When I explained this to him, his eyes got big. "Wow, I get it," he said. "I thought I just sucked, that I was a coward. No wonder I never approached, even though I wanted to so badly. It was like I had a foot on the gas and a foot on the brakes." Jeff is no coward. He was just letting clashing values get the better of him.

GOOD INTENTIONS, BAD OUTCOMES

Problems don't only arise when your top values duke it out with your fear of Rejection. Conflicts can happen *within* your values, like bickering ballplayers on the same team. (Think Jeter and A-Rod going at it.)

Take my Big Three values, from back when I first started approaching women.

1. Growth/Self-Improvement
2. Certainty/Comfort
3. Love/Connection

Now, those look good on paper, but do you see the inherent conflict? My top two values were incompatible. I badly wanted to grow, but I also wanted to stay comfortable. That's like trying to hone six-pack abs without doing crunches.

I fought this internal struggle *for years* without knowing why I felt this way. I wanted to improve at approaching, but when I saw a beautiful woman, my need for certainty meant that to talk to her, I had to perceive a high chance of success—she pretty much had to be alone, smiling, and holding a sign that read "Horny 4 Gingers." So I rarely approached, and then I would castigate myself for not "manning up." I wanted that sure thing, but nothing is certain except death, taxes, and sucky Adam Sandler movies.

I was playing it safe, which is a great value if you're looking at long-term mutual funds, but it won't help you step up to the sexiest woman in the club.

This internal tug-of-war tortured me. I remember a night out in San Diego's Gaslamp Quarter when I spent three hours trying to approach but didn't talk to a single woman. I was so frustrated that when I got back to my hotel, I repeatedly banged my head against the elevator wall. *Thunk, thunk, thunk!* (The wall won.)

UPGRADE YOUR VALUES

The great news? Your Big Three values are not etched in granite. You can upgrade them.

So, what values should you apply in your love life? Use what I call the Five Super-Values. Applying these will change your dating results by changing what you feel, what you focus on, and what actions you take. These values are like an eight-cylinder engine that propels you toward the confidence and romantic connection that you want, and they're a much-needed update to what you've been using.

THE FIVE SUPER-VALUES THAT
CREATE ROMANTIC CONNECTIONS

AUTHENTICITY: Aligning your thoughts, words, and actions from a true, genuine place, and letting women see the real you.

CONNECTION: You don't attract women—they already like you. If you try to attract, you'll repel. But if you try to connect, you'll attract.

COURAGE: Approaching, going for the kiss, speaking genuine thoughts—it takes courage.

FUN/PLAYFULNESS: Abs are overrated. Sculpt a six-pack sense of fun and playfulness. Give women good emotions. To quote the great philosopher Cyndi Lauper: "Girls, they wanna have fun."

RESILIENCE: Tenacity, grit, determination. If connecting with women were easy, every guy would already have his dream girlfriend. It takes resilience.

Note that there are no conflicts within the five Super-Values. They dovetail to help you feel more confident and take better actions. And you can call on any of these values depending on the situation. You might see an attractive woman you want to meet and say, *Okay, time for courage.* You could be on a flatlining first date and realize, *I'm boring her. I need to be more playful.* When the girl you've been messaging goes quiet, you say to yourself, *Be resilient*, and send her one more charming text, instead of giving up too soon.

The night I met Nora, I needed all five Super-Values. I wouldn't have met her without the resilience to give myself that Travis Bickle, bathroom-mirror pep talk. I was authentic with her, and because she likes nerdy writers, we connected. I also needed courage, both to invite her back to my room and to go for the kiss. And along the way, I was fun and playful.

Now, I'm not saying you should retire all of your old values. Just make sure these Super-Values are in the starting lineup.

You might be asking, "Coach, how do I apply these values in a practical way?"

The answer: Play by some new rules.

THE NEW "RULES" OF YOUR LOVE LIFE

There's something just as important as values: your rules. Every value you have comes with one or more "rules" that you've unconsciously written for yourself. You don't know they're there, but you definitely feel their effects on your emotional state. Rules act as triggers—they're what must happen in order for you to experience, feel, or embody a given value.

To use a non-dating example, let's say you value Fitness, and you feel absolutely ripped when you pump iron. The rule in your psychology is, "When I lift, I feel fit and healthy." And let's say that heading home from the gym, a Dodge Durango cuts you off, and you flip the driver the bird. Your road rage stems from a rule that says, "When I get cut off in traffic, I feel anger."

Your mind works the same way in your dating life. For example, if Feeling Attractive/Sexy is an important value to you, your rule may be, "When a woman tells me I'm handsome, I feel sexy." You also come up with rules for when you face the dreaded Rejection. It may be, "When I ask a woman out and she says no, I feel rejected." Or, "When she doesn't text me back, I've been rejected."

Rules for your values activate good feelings. Rules for Rejection activate bad feelings.

The thing is, it's highly likely that your current rules make it *hard* for you to feel good and *easy* for you to feel rejected—which makes dating suck. Why? Most of your rules are probably either outside of your control and/ or hard to achieve. And your rules for feeling Rejection are likely plentiful, covering your dating life like dozens of land mines.

Because you're reading this book, you no doubt value Romantic Success. Your rule might be, "When my date and I make out, I'll feel like a romantic success." Now, you should *totally* enjoy locking lips. But that's not an ideal success criterion because kissing is outside of your control. It takes two, baby. Hard-to-achieve rules make it hard to feel good. (I know this because I used to believe that if I went on a date and we didn't make out, then I'd failed.)

But what if your rule for Romantic Success was easy to achieve and totally in your control? Maybe something like, "Anytime I give my date a flirty compliment, I'll feel like a success." And what if you had lots of rules like that? You'd feel better emotions and enjoy dating more—and that would make you more attractive to women.

Here are the three keys to writing rules for your values:

- They should make it easy to feel good.
- They should be fully in your control.
- Each value should have several rules, any one of which lets you experience that value.

Let's say you most want to feel the value of Confidence. Here's a bad rule: "When I get a kiss, I'll feel confident." (Again, enjoy that kiss! Just don't *need* it to feel confident.) Here's a good rule: "Anytime I go for a kiss, I'll feel confident." Instead of tying your good juju to external outcomes, you're now experiencing those values via your actions. That's incredibly empowering because you can largely control your actions. You're also conditioning yourself to fall in love with the process rather than just the outcome. And the sooner you fall in love with the process, the sooner you'll fall in love with your dream girl (and she with you).

Now, as for Rejection, you're about to adopt my Universal Rejection Rule. Think of it as a firewall that protects your mental software from indulging in this toxic state. (I should note that the goal here is not to totally eradicate feeling rejected. You're human! You're allowed to be bummed if a girl isn't into you. But you want to minimize that pain and refocus on your Amazing Outcome.)

Here's your Universal Rejection Rule, with the key phrases underlined.

"I'll only feel Rejection if I indulge in the <u>illusion</u> that a woman whom I barely know can reject me, <u>instead of remembering</u> that there are a <u>million more girls, and I have more to give</u>."

This rule *rules*. It calls bullshit on "the illusion" that someone who doesn't know you can "reject" you. And the phrase "instead of remembering" shifts your mind to the abundance of dating options that you do have and the abundance of love that you offer.

Dating sucks for tons of men because of Rejection—they see it as a Pandora's Box of painful emotions. This rule locks the box, reminding you that you have endless options and so much to give.

Jeff, the Army veteran who battled approach anxiety, made this his mantra. Armed with this new rule—and his Five Super-Values—he went out on the town and approached more than twenty women. He got "rejected" several times, but his new rule helped him brush those off. He also got a phone full of numbers and made out with a total cutie on the dance floor.

THE REWRITE STUFF

In your missions for this chapter, you'll be rewriting your rules for your Super-Values. Here's the structure to use.

"Anytime I [action you can control], I feel/embody [positive value]."

Here are some of my rules:

- "Anytime I approach an attractive woman as the real me, I feel Authentic."
- "Anytime I go for the first kiss on a date even when I'm afraid, I embody Courage."
- "Anytime I ask a woman a question about her passions and interests, I feel like I'm Connecting."

Check out my old Big Three values and corresponding rules. Notice how hard I was making it to feel good, and how easy it was for me to feel bad.

CONNELL'S OLD VALUES AND RULES

1. **Growth/Self-Improvement**
   Rule: "I feel like I'm growing only when I get 'results' like make-outs, compliments, sex . . ."

2. **Certainty/Comfort**
   Rules: "I only take action when there's a high probability of success . . . ," "I only talk to women who look 'approach-able' . . ."

3. **Love/Connection**
   Rule: "I'm only truly connecting if we get physical . . ."

And behold! Here are my new rules for each Super-Value. Again, I don't need to follow all of these rules—any of them will let me experience these amazing states.

CONNELL'S SUPER-VALUES AND RULES

1. **Authenticity**
   Rules: "I feel authentic anytime I say a deep truth that I feel in the moment (OR) pay her an honest compliment (OR) show my vulnerable side (OR) tell a story that's not intended to impress (OR) share an opinion she might not like or agree with (OR) tell her something I find cool or sexy about her . . ."

2. **Connection**
   Rules: "I feel connected to a woman anytime I listen hard to what she's saying (OR) try to find out what makes her tick (OR) look for commonalities (OR) say something flirtatious (OR) empathize with something she shared with me . . ."

3. **Courage**

    Rules: "I feel courageous anytime I compliment a woman (OR) approach a woman I consider intimidatingly sexy (OR) go for the kiss on a date (OR) send a flirty text (OR) invite a woman to come home with me . . ."

4. **Fun/Playfulness**

    Rules: "I feel fun and playful anytime I crack a joke (OR) try to make my date smile (OR) sing karaoke (OR) play a fun first-date game like Two Lies and a Truth . . ."

5. **Resilience**

    Rules: "I feel resilient anytime I want to quit approaching but decide to keep going (OR) send one more text to a woman who didn't write me back instead of giving up (OR) go to the gym even when I don't want to (OR) get 'rejected' by a woman and approach a new one in less than five seconds . . ."

As for Rejection, I used to have so many opportunities to feel it: When a date didn't want to kiss me; when a woman didn't text me back right away; when I approached and she wasn't interested. And on and on.

Now, I live by this Universal Rejection Rule:

"I'll only feel Rejection if I indulge in the illusion that a woman I barely know can reject me, instead of remembering that there are a million more girls, and I have more to give."

This mindset makes it much easier to approach, to take chances, and to enjoy dating.

CHAPTER 4 MISSIONS
....

Three Steps to Clarifying Your Values and Defeating Your Fear of Rejection

1. **Assess Your Current Values and Rules**

    List your Big Three values that have guided your dating life up to now and the rules you've been applying. How have you been making it harder to enjoy dating and connecting with women?

2. **Write Three New Rules for Each Super-Value**
    You now have Five Super-Values. Write *at least* three rules for each, making sure you follow the structure provided. Write a minimum of fifteen total rules—three for each Super-Value.

3. **Read Your Universal Rejection Rule Every Day**
    Say it, learn it, love it: "I'll only feel Rejection if I indulge in the illusion that a woman I barely know can reject me, instead of remembering that there are a million more girls, and I have more to give."

SO WHAT HAVE WE LEARNED?

- Your values are the hidden forces that govern your dating results.
- Five Super-Values will help catapult you toward your Amazing Outcome.
- Your rules should be easy to achieve and in your control.
- The Universal Rejection Rule takes the sting out of Rejection.
- Elevator walls are a lot harder than they look.
- You're more than enough. Never forget that.

That wraps up your mindset work. Does your brain hurt? Be proud. Why? Because psychology counts for a full 80 percent of the puzzle pieces you need in place for a great dating life. Techniques are a blast, but they only make up 20 percent of success.

That said, it's time for the fun stuff. You're about to get the secret weapon that will make you magnetic to women, smash you out of the friend zone, and get girls chasing you.

SUCCESS STORIES

Here are three clients who solved their biggest dating problems by using Super-Values and rewriting their rules.

THE END OF THE FRIEND ZONE

CHRIS ("Chris Cross"), thirty-four, software developer

PROBLEM: Friend zone

GAME-CHANGING SUPER-VALUE: Playfulness

NEW RULE: "Anytime I crack a joke that loosens me up, I'll feel playful and fun."

SUCCESS STORY: Chris was going on lots of Tinder dates but couldn't land a second date. He realized he was putting himself in the friend zone by being too safe and not flirting, for fear of getting rejected and feeling creepy. His new rules loosened him up, which relaxed him and made it easier for him to flirt. Two of his next three dates included hot-and-heavy make-outs, and he soon had an awesome girlfriend.

APPROACHING WITH CONFIDENCE

MARTIN ("Mighty Martin"), twenty-seven, website designer

PROBLEM: Approach anxiety

GAME-CHANGING SUPER-VALUE: Courage

NEW RULE: "Anytime I approach a pretty girl who gives me butterflies, I embody courage."

SUCCESS STORY: A pretty blonde caught Martin's eye as he was perusing nonfiction titles at his local bookstore. He felt the butterflies but no anxiety, using courage to approach and say, "Hi. You're adorable and I had to meet you." Her eyes lit up, and five minutes later they swapped numbers to set up a date. "Amazing," Martin said. "I felt weightless."

MORE MATCHES, MORE DATES, MORE FUN

SAM ("Scooter"), fifty-four, beer distributor

PROBLEM: Lonely/lack of dates

GAME-CHANGING SUPER-VALUES: Authentic Expression and Fun/Playfulness

NEW RULE: "Anytime I send a funny message on Match, I feel authentic and attractive."

SUCCESS STORY: Sam was putting off launching a dating-app profile. His fear? That he'd get no interest, making him feel old and unattractive. By embracing Authentic Expression and Fun/Playfulness—that one was easy, since Sam is super funny—he felt attractive and smashed through that conflict. He realized Rejection was just in his head. Two days after launching his profile, he had nine women blowing up his in-box and was going on three dates a week.

HOW TO IGNITE ROMANTIC CONNECTION

> Be still when you have nothing to say; when genuine passion
> moves you, say what you've got to say, and say it hot.
> —D. H. Lawrence, *Studies in Classic American Literature*[1]

....

As he sat in the candlelit wine bar waiting for Becca to arrive, Trevor could feel the nerves churn. It was their first date, and he was excited to meet the successful chef he'd connected with on Bumble. She wasn't just a beautiful brunette; she was quick and witty, matching him text for clever text.

But Trevor had been struggling with first dates. He'd met several women recently and none of them had felt a strong connection. And on a quick pre-date phone call, Becca gave him a heads-up: "With the last couple guys I met, there was no chemistry, so don't take it personally if we don't hit it off." A preemptive friend-zoning?

"It's like I'm in Alcatraz," said Trevor (Higher Self name: "Clever Trevor").

This night would be different, though, because Trevor had been honing his Man-to-Woman Communication—a turbocharged form of flirting that amplifies romantic connection. Becca walked in and found Trevor to be warm and roguish, while he was impressed by her easy confidence. He gently teased her for running a few minutes behind schedule ("You owe me a drink for every minute you were late"), and she laughed. Trevor gave her space, not leaning in too much or seeming overly eager. And he was playful, a trait that had been lacking in her recent dates. When Becca looked at his button-down shirt, he feigned offense. "My eyes are up *here*," he said. "Please stop objectifying me." She giggled and punched his arm.

They bonded over their passions for cooking and yoga. During their second drink, Trevor took her hand and intertwined their fingers, and Becca tossed her leg over his. He moved closer and whispered in her ear: "You're even cooler than I was hoping." Minutes later, they were kissing, with half the bar shooting them *Get a room* glances. Before they left, she suggested their next get-together—a private couple's massage at her favorite spa. Not a bad second date. Walking home, Trevor felt a heady buzz of romance, Belgian beer, and freedom. He had finally escaped from Alcatraz.

When sparks fly between two people, it can seem random—something that "just happens," like a lightning strike or winning the Powerball. But the truth is, you can learn to consistently ignite that romantic connection using Man-to-Woman Communication—the breezy, flirty frequency that amplifies natural chemistry. It's a one-way ticket to romantic connection, as well as the lens through which you can (and should) channel all of the interactions in your love life—your texts, your approaches, and your dates.

In this chapter, I'll break down the art of Man-to-Woman Communication (M-W). I'll also share twenty-one practical methods that you can apply in your dating life. If you've ever wondered, *How do I talk to girls and get them into me?* you're about to learn the answers here.

THE END OF THE FRIEND ZONE

Imagine you're on a first date, but it's going nowhere fast. She checks her phone a lot, the conversation is polite and platonic, and after one drink she says, "I have to run, but it was nice meeting you." Heading home you think, *What did I do wrong? Am I just not attractive?*

Now, let's say you're on a date with that same woman, but this time the air is electric. She twirls her hair and touches your arm, and you feel magnetic. You lean in and kiss her. You know there will be a second date—and who knows where this night may lead.

The difference between these two scenes: In the first, you played it safe and treated her like a friendly acquaintance. In the second, you let go, loosened up, and connected on the Man-to-Woman wavelength.

So in reality, women don't put us in the friend zone—we do it to ourselves! How? By treating them like buddies and not as potential lovers.

TURN THE CHANNEL

All social interactions have a particular "frame"—an unspoken set of behavioral cues and assumptions that determines its context and governs the way people relate to one another. Almost every interaction you have with others (apart from family members) falls into one of three frames:

Friend-to-Friend: A purely platonic vibe, with no sexual subtext.

Man-to-Woman: A romantic context in which your masculine side and a woman's feminine essence click.

Patron-to-Professional/Business: The way you relate to colleagues, clients, or the staff at, say, restaurants and shops.

Almost every encounter you have with a woman will fall into one of these frames. It's how the mind makes sense of social situations. We automatically click to one of these three "channels," as if wielding a TV remote.

Dating problems arise when you inadvertently select the Friend-to-Friend channel while with a woman you're into, rather than flipping to M-W. A girl may find you attractive, but your subcommunications and social cues—your vibe, voice, and eye contact, among other influences—make her feel, *I'm not into him.* Hello, friend zone.

Here are the three primary pillars of being Man-to-Woman:

1. **Showing Clear Interest**
   Your words and actions let her know you're romantically interested—that this is the story of boy meets girl, not friend meets friend.

2. **Communicating Emotionally, Not Logically**
   Most men naturally communicate in a logical, analytical way, but that stifles romantic connection. M-W is an emotional language.

3. **Leading, Not Following**
   Dating is like dancing, and that means as the man, you usually lead. You lead the conversation, you ask her out, you pick the place, you steer the conversation.

On his prior dates, Trevor hadn't shown enough clear interest, was speaking on a logical (rather than emotional) wavelength, and he wasn't leading enough. (He often left it to his dates to pick the location and set up plans.) But with Becca, he made some important changes. He chose the venue, and she liked his taking charge. He teased her, and she laughed. He told her that she's pretty, and she blushed. He led the conversation, held her hand, went for the first kiss—and each time she followed his lead. This heightened their attraction, and soon sparks became a brushfire.

Man, woman. Action, reaction.

He turned the dial straight to Man-to-Woman, which is like going from whatever's on PBS to *Fifty Shades of Grey* (but your dates will have way better dialogue).

NOTHING BUT MAMMALS

I used to be terrified to show women my romantic interest. I didn't want to be "that creepy guy" who hits on girls. But one of my coaches drummed this mantra into me: "I make no apologies for my desires as a man."

Buy into this. There's nothing wrong or creepy about wanting love, sex, and connection. It's healthy and normal. Humans crave companionship. It's natural. As the song says, we ain't nothin' but mammals. In fact, I believe the key to reaching your potential as a fulfilled, authentic man means getting in touch with and embracing your sexual side, while still remaining the awesome, classy guy that you are at your core.

And Mother Nature is a helluva wing-gal. You see, attraction is automatic when respective core energies meet. When there's polarity between two people's energies, proverbial sparks fly. The more polarity, the stronger the attraction.

Communicating on the Friend-to-Friend frequency with a date can depolarize sexual tension, dousing potential embers with a bucket of water.

"YOU'RE LOOKING
AT ME LIKE I'M DESSERT"
....

You don't need a lot of attraction "tactics." Too many moves can make you come off as fake or try-hard, which pushes women away. The Hulk doesn't need a handgun. Just letting your authentic interest show can be enough.

During a trip to L.A., I met Valerie, an ambitious women's-fashion expert. For our first date, we had drinks at a patio bar in Venice Beach, near my hotel. We seemed very different on paper. Her: a Black woman who went from an inner-city upbringing to owning a Santa Monica boutique. Me: a privileged white guy from the Midwestern burbs. But our M-W polarity was off the charts. We both felt the sexual tension rising as we teased, talked, and laughed. At one point, my wolfish eye contact made her say, "You're looking at me like I'm dessert." As we walked back to my hotel, she was unbuttoning her top before I had my key in the door.

A big piece of the M-W puzzle is speaking to women on an emotional wavelength. Men occupy the logical, analytical world of the masculine, but women respond to emotions. Research backs this up. A landmark 1995 Yale study found that, in general, men and women use different spheres of the brain, concluding that men are more logical-minded and fact-based, while women feel their emotions more strongly.[3]

When dating, seek to channel a more visceral, emotional side. Women are drawn to the language of feelings and meaning, rather than dry facts and information. Often a cool, attractive guy is friend-zoned when his communication is too logical, so for her there's no spark. It's a date, not a business lunch. You want to filter your language through an emotional lens, not a logical one. Be Captain Kirk, not Mr. Spock. (You might have noticed there's a paradox at play here. To create the romantic connection you want, you need to embody masculine qualities while also accessing the feminine realm of emotions. More on that in the next chapter.)

Here are two brief, mini-bios of me that contain the same information. In the first, it's just the facts. In the second, I use language that's descriptive and emotionally evocative, and I've underlined the key phrases.

LOGICAL: "I've lived in New York City for twenty years. I moved here to be a writer. I'm now a dating coach. I also play tennis, sing karaoke, and read books about the Civil War."

EMOTIONAL: "I've lived in New York City for twenty wild, fulfilling years. I moved here to follow my dream of being a writer. I'm a dating coach, which lights me up because I help men and women find love. When I'm not throwing my racket like a brat on the tennis court, I sing eighties power ballads on karaoke nights and nerd out on Civil War books."

The logical description is dry (I almost dozed off typing it), while the latter has life and heart. I'm hardly the most charismatic guy in the world, but women who like my type find me very attractive in part because I can speak the language of emotions.

"SPIKE" THE INTERACTION

As you'll learn shortly, there are countless fun, effective ways to turn on the M-W channel. But in terms of the basic structure, there are only three parts. Remembering these will help you keep things simple when chatting and flirting.

1. **Baseline Communication:** You being sincere, real, chill, vulnerable. Just sharing your honest thoughts and feelings. This is a low bar. No need to be funny or witty. If you can hold a conversation with another human, you're good!

2. **Positive Spikes:** Compliments, flirty comments, physical expressiveness (touching, kissing), jokes, commonalities, shared passions—anything that "spikes" her emotions in a positive sense.

3. **Negative Spikes:** Not "negative" in a Debbie Downer way, but rather teasing, busting her chops, challenging her in ways she enjoys (basically, it's pulling her pigtails), which complement the Positive Spikes.

In conversations with women, you'll spend most of your time in Baseline Communication, feeling no pressure to be funny or charismatic. In fact, you can be borderline boring. It won't be an issue because every so often you'll throw in a Positive Spike or a Negative Spike to stimulate both of your emotions and keep it exciting.

A MAN-TO-WOMAN INTERACTION

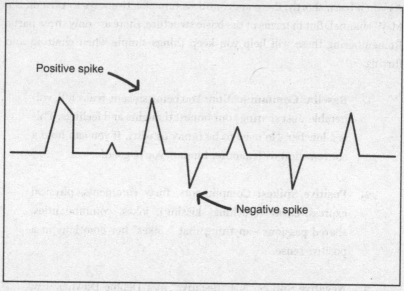

From texting to approaching to first dates, your ideal interaction will blend positive spikes (such as compliments) and a few negative spikes (playful teasing) with lots of normal conversation. You give the woman a fun, emotional ride while being authentic.

Not only will you not bore her, but your relaxed, easy vibe will make those emotional spikes—the teases, compliments, and emotional high points—all the more powerful. And you don't want too many spikes, or else you'll seem try-hard and not relatable.

To find the right balance, think of an EKG heartbeat monitor. The Baseline that runs horizontally represents your "normal" conversation—just your sincere self. And the peaks and valleys are the Positive and Negative Spikes that occur in the moment. As with this image, most of the time you'll be in Baseline. Also, you'll likely want more Positive than Negative Spikes. The Negatives are more powerful and should be used sparingly, depending on your personality and what your date responds to (e.g., some women *love* being teased—others, not so much).

And here's what a friend-zone date looks like: a flatlining EKG that's all Baseline. It's just boring, logical conversation. (Get the pads, stat!)

UH-OH! FRIEND ZONE!

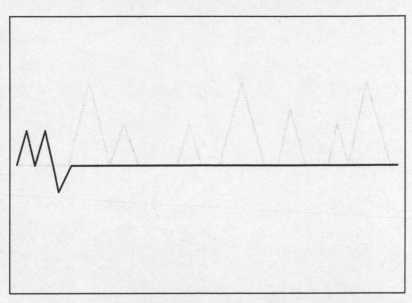

Get the crash pads. Your typical go-nowhere date looks like this: Your communication is safe, logical, and dull. There are few emotional spikes, leaving her less than stimulated. This is what makes women text, "You seem great, but I didn't feel a spark."

Alternatively, an interaction can have way too many Positive and zero Negative Spikes. This happens when you try to win her approval by being super nice and ass-kissing.

A BIT TOO UPBEAT

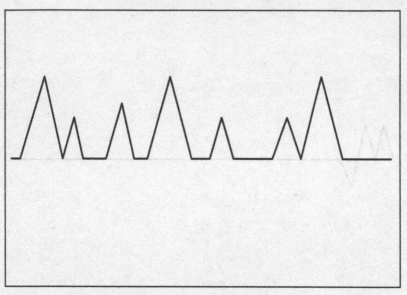

Positivity is important, but beware of having too many of these spikes ("You're amazing! You're beautiful!"). It's inauthentic and can make you seem overly eager.

TWENTY-ONE WAYS
TO BE MAN-TO-WOMAN

Here are twenty-one tools at your disposal when interacting with a woman you're attracted to. Pro tip: Less is more! Don't go on a date with a huge list of "moves" to unleash. Women like you for you. These are the icing, not the cake.

1. **Show Clear Interest**
   If you're interested in a woman, make it clear. It can be as simple as saying, "Let's go on a date," rather than "Let's hang out." On the date, don't hide your feelings. Tell her or show her that you think she's sexy or cool. Clarity helps you set the M-W frame.

2. **Talk the Talk**

The way you use your voice conveys your confidence level, so cultivate a rich, resonant tonality. Record conversations with a friend and listen to your voice for flaws such as "uptalking" (when statements sound like questions) and excessive *ums* and *uhs*. When speaking to someone, imagine another person is directly behind them and talk loud enough that both of them can hear you. This will help you project your voice, since chances are your voice shuts down a little when speaking to a woman you find attractive. (It's a common unconscious reaction when we feel insecure.)

Think of a continuum of voice tonality, from supplicating (hesitant, quiet, uptalking) to neutral/friendly (your normal voice) to commanding (drill sergeant barking orders). Seek the sweet spot between commanding and neutral/friendly. This is the tonality that sounds firm and certain, yet friendly and upbeat.

Commanding
Sweet spot that women like ←
Neutral/Friendly
Supplicating

3. **Assume M-W Body Language**

Stand tall, widen your stance a bit, and take up space. When you stand, imagine that your spine is a steel rod. Powerful body language not only sends women the right message— it boosts your emotional state. Try it right now: Stand up, hunch your shoulders, touch your ankles together, and hold that pose for thirty seconds. You feel small and passive, right? Okay, now stand *tall*, like your spine is made of steel, push your shoulders back, take a wide stance, and hold this pose for thirty seconds. I bet you feel more confident and masculine. That's because adopting a "dominant" body language can increase your testosterone and reduce cortisol, the stress hormone.

4. Look Her in the Eye

I dated a marketing director named Olivia, whom I'd met at Whole Foods. On our first date, I asked her what she liked about my approach, thinking she'd mention my smooth "pickup line." But women rarely remember your opening words. "That's easy," she said. "You looked me in the eye."

5. Be Physically Expressive

Physical expressiveness is a simple, powerful way to create an M-W vibe. You can high-five, hold her hand, tap her arm, touch her thigh, whisper in her ear, or brush the hair from her eyes, among other ways—assuming, of course, that she's made it clear that she's comfortable with this, is enjoying it, and also reciprocates. If you've gotten the "green light," this is okay to do, within boundaries. We're humans. We touch. And for some women, physical touch is the main way they experience love and connection.

You want to be physically expressive in a way that makes her feel safe and comfortable. To help do this, have a reason for the physical contact. Just randomly touching her is weird. Make it an extension of your words and/or the emotion of the moment.

- "What? You love Coldplay, too? Up high!" [*High-five*]
- "I have a secret to tell you . . ." [*Lean in, whisper in her ear*]
- "Your favorite movie is *The Mighty Ducks*? You need to go now." [*Lightly push her away*]

Begin with small touches and taps on her arm or upper elbow. This gets her comfortable with your physicality, and lets you see if she likes it or not. (If she clearly doesn't like it or if you're just not sure, then stop.) It also gives her the opportunity to reciprocate, such as when Becca tossed her leg over Trevor's.

Physical expression is the stairway to intimacy with

a woman you have chemistry with. Women *hate* a handsy, octopus-armed creep. But in general, they love a man who's comfortable being physically expressive while being aware of how she's responding. (In the chapter on great first dates, I'll elaborate on this crucial difference.)

6. **Approach with a Power Compliment**

When you approach, a fantastic way to start a conversation is to pay her a Power Compliment. It should be three things: sincere, specific, and not about her physical attributes. Does she have a cool tattoo? Stylish leather boots? An awesome Springsteen T-shirt? Tell her what you noticed and why you're impressed. ("I love Bruce, too. He was my first concert.")

7. **Tease Her**

Light, playful teasing can amplify attraction. So if you're a natural ballbuster, like I am, tease her a bit and see if she responds well. Avoid areas that could bring offense, like her appearance, family, job, or pets. (I once called a woman's dog a "little rat," and she almost got up and left.) Stick to less touchy topics like her taste in movies, TV shows, or music.

8. **Use the Push-Pull**

Teases and compliments are both effective tools. A "push-pull" combines one of each. The positive comment "pulls" her closer to you, while the tease playfully "pushes" her away.

- Push: Playfully showing disinterest.
- Pull: Showing interest.
- Push-Pull: A light, joking comment that blends both.

It works because the contrast of the positive and negative creates a compelling, surprising curiosity. It makes the brain happy. (The title of this book is a push-pull: *Dating Sucks,*

[push] *but You Don't* [pull].) A push-pull gives her an emotionally layered experience. It's two great tastes that taste great together—the Reese's Cup of flirting.

Here are some push-pull examples:

- "You're either the coolest girl I've met in a while or the nerdiest. I'm just not sure which one yet."
- "I was falling for you until you said [comment she made]."
- "You're so cute—you remind me of my little sister."
- "We should go on a date, as long as you promise not to stalk me."

Avoid using rehearsed push-pulls; the best ones arise in the moment. And when you get good, you can stack several into a conversation. Many guys are afraid to flirt and to tease a girl. A push-pull lets you do both, dialing up romantic tension.

9. **Flirt, Don't Fawn**
My former dating coach Anthony Recenello helped to show me the difference between flirting with women and fawning over them. An easy mistake to make is fawning—being too impressed by a woman too quickly. Such comments might include, "You are just so amazing," "I've never met anyone like you," and "Wow, you are so beautiful!" Those things are fine to say after you've gotten close, but if you lay it on too thick too soon, you can come across as her groupie, not her equal. That's a big turn-off.

So don't fawn. Flirt. I define flirting as showing a woman that she's affecting you but in a casual, no-big-deal way. This makes her feel sexy and attractive, without putting her on a pedestal. Here are examples of being affected by her but not fawning over her.

- "Sorry, what did you say? Your lips were distracting me."
- "That dress is very . . . *wow*. Anyway . . ."
- [*After she says something you approve of*] "That makes me want to make out with you, but I'll try to behave myself."

To see a master flirt in action, watch clips of comedian Craig Ferguson on his old CBS talk show, *The Late Late Show*. Whenever a beautiful starlet was his guest, he always let his attraction show with humor and class, and he never fawned.

10. Change Her Mood, Not Her Mind

If an interaction isn't going the way you'd like, change her mood, not her mind. That is, don't use logic. Try humor or storytelling or try to tease her. Spike the interaction.

For a few weeks, I had been trying for a first date with Annie—a kind, curious, private-equity real estate agent I'd connected with on The League, a members-only dating app. We couldn't get our schedules aligned. One day she sent me a polite blow-off message. I used M-W, and only a few messages after seeming to reject me, she called *me* to set up a date. Here's how I did it.

ANNIE: Hey, sorry I won't be able to meet you. I am talking to someone else about a first date. But best of luck.

ME: No worries at all. Glad to hear you made a love connection. But I'll have to return the engagement ring I bought you. ♂

ANNIE: Lol. Sorry I'm just an honest person . . . But hey, perhaps it will be a terrible date.

ME: I have an idea. How about I come on the date with you! & you can give the guy you like most a rose, like on the *Bachelorette*.

ANNIE: Lol! That would be different fer sure. It's too bad

that you and I never connected. I just don't like dating more than one guy.

ME: No worries. I only spent $7 on your ring so it's OK. A fake diamond. Diamond-oid.

ANNIE: Perfect. I'm clumsy and I probably would fall and lose the ring.

ME: Phew! Then I dodged a bullet. I mean, you're adorable and you seem cool, but if you dropped the symbol of our eternal love down in the gutter, that would hurt. 💔

ANNIE: LMAO. I can't help it. I'm clumsy.

ME: That is SO you. It's why I proposed.

ANNIE: Hahaha. You're cute. Maybe I should meet you.

ME: Lol. Thanks. You're suuuper cute. I'm just trying to keep up. You have a great sense of humor. & Don't worry. I never propose till date no 2.

ANNIE: Haha. We should meet up. Imma call you in a min . . .

Seconds later, my phone rang, we talked for a half hour, and we had a great date three nights later that ended with her spending the night. And all I did was have fun by cracking dumb jokes, rather than try to logically convince her to meet with me, which would not have worked.

To change her mind, change her mood.

11. Text a Woman as You Would a Good Friend

Grab your phone and find a recent text exchange with a good friend. I'll bet your tone with your pal is relaxed and light, maybe with a joke or good-natured jibe tossed in, right? This is because you're being authentic, not trying to impress. You want to text a woman the same way, but with a little M-W sprinkled in.

12. Add a Dash of Cockiness

Back in the day, I spent more time in the friend zone than Jerry Rice spent in the end zone. Adding a dash of cockiness helped me escape. I'm a natural-born smart-ass, but I was hiding that side of me on dates. So when I met Amy on Match, I let that snarky side come out. On our first date, I teased her, accusing her of checking out my (nonexistent) ass. The next day, I texted, "I just want you to know that you had a great time last night and you'd like to see me again." She loved it. Our chemistry was like fireworks on the Fourth. If you have a cheeky side, let women see it. Just make sure you combine cocky comments with humor, or else you can come across as pompous.

13. Compliment Her Inner Qualities

We all want to be appreciated for what's inside. Let a woman know an inner quality you like about her. Are you impressed by her smarts, wits, sense of humor, or caring heart? Tell her. Lots of guys have told her how beautiful she is on the outside. Be that rare man who also sees the beauty within.

14. Give Her a "Deal Breaker"

A fun way to spike a date is to take an innocent detail about her and pretend—playfully, of course—that it's a deal breaker.

HER: I'm more of a cat person than a dog person.

YOU: What? No! That's a deal breaker. I knew you were too good to be true.

HER: No, I like dogs! I just love cats more.

YOU: Sorry, I don't think I can be with someone who has a coat made of Dalmatians.

HER: [laughing] No, I really do love dogs.

In addition to generating fun banter, giving your date little challenges can make her "chase" you a bit, getting her more invested in winning you over. And it's a truism that the more invested in something a person is, the more they want that something.

15. Move Your Eyes in a "7" Pattern

To dial up the sexual tension, move your eyes in a "7" pattern— that is, from her right eye to her left eye and down to her lips. This will amplify your attraction to her, which can enhance something called "emotional state transference." Emotions are contagious—what you feel, a woman will feel. If you let yourself get lost in her baby blues, you can transfer the desire that you feel onto her.

16. Say the Scary Thing

We're all searching for truth and realness, so get in the habit of sharing scary but honest feelings with women—as long as it's not vulgar or negative, of course. This emotional naked- ness can be powerful, and by going first, you free your date to do the same. Such phrases often start out like this:

- "You know what I like about you . . ."
- "Here's what scares me the most . . ."
- "I want to share something with you, but I'm not sure if I should . . ."

To be extra brave, say one of the above phrases to your next date without knowing how you'll finish the thought! As long as you're being honest and present, your brain will fig- ure out the "right words," and your date will know that they're real.

17. Give Her a Nickname

"Troublemaker." "Kiddo." "Freckles." Giving a nickname to someone means you know and like them, and it suggests familiarity. The night I met my future girlfriend Carrie, she started calling me "Ginger-Man," and it made me even more into her. (Damn, this stuff works on me, too!)

18. Make *Her* the Seducer

I love to misinterpret an innocent comment as "evidence" that my date wants to seduce me. A lot of women love this. By flipping the male-female dynamic and accusing her of objectifying you, you subtly tell her, *I'm not like those guys.* Also, it takes things from a logical, Friend-to-Friend context to M-W. And it's just fun.

HER: I recently redid my bedroom . . .

YOU: Listen, I'm not going to bed with you tonight. I know I'm sexy, but we just met, so let's take it slow.

Look for opportunities to say the kinds of things to women that women always tell horned-up guys. (As a joke! You're not actually accusing her of anything.) Some examples . . .

- "Umm, my eyes are up here."
- "Just so you know, I don't hold hands until the third date."
- "Stop trying to kiss me—I'm a gentleman, not a piece of meat."

Bonus: Some women enjoy this role reversal so much that they fully commit to the seducer role, insisting that you go back to her place, or that you take her to yours. And it's just not gentlemanly to say no to a lady.

19. Be the Buyer, Not the Seller

Men often try to "sell" themselves to women they've just met, which can come across as desperate. It's better to adopt a buyer-seller vibe, with you as the buyer. If you're at a Best Buy shopping for a new TV, you don't try to convince the salesman that a certain model is right for you, and you don't try to impress him. First you see if the TV is what you're looking for. In the same respect, find out if a woman meets your standards. This keeps you from appearing overly eager. Be the buyer.

20. Tell Personal Stories

We're hardwired to love stories. A good anecdote from your life makes you more charismatic, holds her interest, and invites her to share her own stories. Here are some storytelling tips.

- Follow a three-part structure: setting, conflict, resolution. Here's a story from my teenage years that I've told on many dates: "I was in study hall in high school [setting] before a geometry test. I knew I wasn't ready, and if I failed I'd end up in summer school [conflict]. So I went to the nurse and pretended to have back spasms. When my parents came, instead of taking me home, they took me to the hospital for X-rays. And the doctor diagnosed me with scoliosis—for fake back spasms! [resolution]"

- Details bring a story to life, making it more vivid. Include lots of specifics.

- Avoid stories meant to make you look "cool." It's much cooler to laugh about an embarrassing moment from your past—say, the time you struck out and lost the game, not the time you hit the home run to win the game. Vulnerability is powerful and attractive. But don't overthink it. Some of the best stories are just weird, funny incidents. My client Craig (Higher Self name: "Mr. Clutch") loves telling his dates about the time his friends snuck him into Canada by rolling him inside of a carpet and putting him in the back of an SUV.

21. Embrace the Essence of the Craft

I worked with a top mental-game coach named Jim Fannin, who's trained elite athletes such as Alex Rodriguez. Fannin teaches a concept called "the essence of the craft." He has top athletes distill complex tasks into one simple phrase so that they don't overthink things. At the plate, A-Rod used to tell himself, *I hit the ball flat with an accelerated bat.*

When you're interacting with a woman, the last thing you need is to try to remember dozens of tips and techniques. To get into the moment and keep things simple, create a short mantra (less than ten words) that captures the essence of the *dating* craft for you. Here's mine. Feel free to steal it.

"Be authentic and make her smile."

If I'm real and can put a smile on her face, there's a great chance for a romantic connection. Plus, this reminder shifts my mind away from my insecurities and doubts—yep, I have them, too—and lets me focus on giving her a great time.

I encourage you to review this list before you go on a date or go out to meet women. But when you're with a girl, keep things simple. Forget these twenty-one tips, and embrace the essence of the craft. The right moves will arise, as needed. Get out of your head and into the moment. Give her the present of your authentic presence.

CHAPTER 5 MISSIONS
....

Four Steps to Get Better at Connecting with Women

1. **Compliment Five Women**
   Give five women sincere, specific compliments, in real life (not online). These can be cashiers, baristas, or women you meet at parties or social events.

2. **Make Your Voice Your Calling Card**
   The tone of your voice conveys confidence, or lack thereof.

Practice speaking with a resonant, assertive tonality. Be like Walt Whitman and sound your barbaric *YAWP*.

3. **Stand Tall and Look Her in the Eyes**
   Practice good posture and eye contact. When you stand, imagine your spine is a steel rod. And when you speak to people in person, notice their eye color.

4. **Test-Drive Three Tips of Your Choice**
   Try three of the twenty-one tips that sound especially appealing to you, from playfully teasing to writing your "essence of the craft" to the push-pull (my personal favorite). And don't worry if you have no dates on the horizon—you can try many of these M-W moves with women you meet in the daily course of your life. But DON'T bring your new bag of tricks to work. I advise against dating at work and even subtly flirting at work. Keep things strictly business when you're doing business.

SO WHAT HAVE WE LEARNED?
....

- Man-to-Woman Communication is your key to escaping the friend zone, and the lens through which you'll channel all of your interactions—from dates to approaches to texting to online dating.
- At its essence, M-W is an emotional frequency, not a logical/analytical one.
- Teases and Negative Spikes are fun, but take a less-is-more approach.
- Captain Kirk got way more action than Spock. Just sayin'.
- Yet another reason why you're enough: You now have twenty-one killer moves in your toolbox.

SIX THINGS A GUY
SHOULD NEVER, EVER DO

Send a Dick Pic: Men should keep their junk in the garage.

Mansplain: This is when a guy explains something to a woman in a condescending manner. A great way to guard against doing this is first asking, "Can I share something with you?" If you get permission, it's explaining, not mansplaining.

Lie About Important Stuff: If a fellow fibs about the number of Boy Scout merit badges he had, no biggie. But when it comes to age, relationship status, and desire (or lack thereof) to have a relationship, men need to be as transparent as glass.

Send Angry Messages After Getting Blown Off or Ghosted: Rejection can hurt. I've been there. (I've seen more ghosts than Jack Nicholson in *The Shining*.) But women are doing their best, just like we are. Never send an angry message. Take the high road. It's good for women and good for a guy's soul.

Expect/Pressure a Woman for Sex: There's a zillion good reasons for a woman not to have sex with a guy, so we should never, ever expect it or pressure a woman for it. Ever.

Be Someone You're Not: Well, unless it's for sexy, consensual role-playing—you know, a naughty game of Pirate and Captive. In which case, enjoy!

CHAPTER 6

ARE YOU MANLY ENOUGH TO BE FEMININE?

> There is nothing noble in being superior to your fellow man;
> true nobility is being superior to your former self.
> —commonly attributed to Ernest Hemingway[1]

....

I love that quote, but it doesn't change the fact that Ernest Hemingway was a huge asshole.

As a younger man, he was vulnerable and shy; Gertrude Stein called him "truly sensitive."[2] He poured that tenderness and feeling into his stories. But as he aged into the macho persona of "Papa," Hemingway betrayed his friends, ignored his kids, beat his wives, and killed rare rhinos and lions. He finally turned his shotgun on himself.

Hemingway is an object lesson in the price that men, women, and society pay for the received idea of masculinity. (Arguably, he's not even the most dickish tough-guy novelist of the twentieth century. Charles Bukowski—whom another well-known male dating expert moons over—wrote a book called *Women*, but he didn't much like women. To see the snarling face of toxic masculinity, find the YouTube clip of Bukowski kicking his future wife and calling her a "fucking cunt."[3])

In the last chapter, I discussed Man-to-Woman Communication and how it helps ignite the natural masculine-feminine polarity. Now, let's explore the power of channeling your feminine side, which is part of being Radically Authentic. Women are attracted to masculine energy. But believe it or not, they're also drawn to a man's softer side.

I stumbled on this insight years ago during a second date. "I hope you're not a wolf in sheep's clothing," Cathy said as we downed smoothies on a park bench. A bright, inquisitive art dealer, she had met her share of jerks. "Actually, I'm a sheep in *wolf's* clothing," I said. I was just trying for a clever turn of phrase, but Cathy's eyes widened. I'd accidentally strummed a power chord inside her. "That's the dream," she said. "A man who's a *man* but also soft inside. That's what we want!"

You may associate femininity with weakness. But embracing that side of yourself doesn't rob you of your masculine essence. It balances it, making you more complex and complete. It helps you get emotionally attuned to others. If you "pay close attention," Carl Jung writes in *The Red Book: Liber Novus*, "you will see that the most masculine man has a feminine soul, and the most feminine woman has a masculine soul."[4]

Yes, a "real man" approaches, leads, and makes moves. But he also empathizes, listens, and shows compassion. And he's kind, a highly attractive quality. Just as you should make no apologies for your masculine desires, you should make no apologies for the more feminine aspects of your nature. *GQ* magazine called empathy "the antidote to toxicity."[5] When you embrace your feminine side, it's easier to empathize—to feel what others feel.

"BE A DICK TO WOMEN"

I know about macho bravado. As I was learning to be a better dater, I tried many different styles and approaches, some of which involved working with pickup artists. One of the "gurus" who coached me had become known in the dating-advice industry for making extreme, polarizing comments to women. His advice to me: "Go out for a month and be a total dick."

Thinking that my nice-guy side might be holding me back, I set out to spend thirty days acting like a jerk to women. I said shocking things and made crass remarks. It didn't work. I felt awful. One woman poured a (well-deserved) pitcher of ice water down my shirt. Two weeks in, I called it quits after a disastrous double date at an upscale Manhattan lounge. My friend Cameron had set me up with a woman of Chinese descent. I cracked a "joke" that included an epithet for Asians, which was met by arctic silence and dropped jaws. I had insulted my date and embarrassed my buddy and myself.

So, I took off the asshole mask for good. Masks don't work.

Sure, women want men of strength, but there's nothing strong about vulgar insults. Real strength is showing vulnerability and true emotion. You can still be a guy's guy, if that's who you are. You can keep your Harley and your bowling nights. Just drop your guard and access your kindness and empathy.

I'm fairly masculine. I shoot hoops, read World War II books, and help guys get girls. But I'm kinda feminine, too. I listen, talk about my feelings, love musical theater, and—no lie—I cried at the end of *My Cousin Vinny*. (Hey, when they win the court case, you really feel it.)

You contain multitudes, and that complexity will be irresistible to women who like your type. In a 2017 University of Glasgow study, women were more attracted to men who balanced both masculine and feminine traits, as opposed to men who were either very masculine or very feminine.[6] Plus, embracing your feminine side can help you become more emotionally expressive. As I explained in the previous chapter, communicating with women on an emotional wavelength—rather than a logical one—is crucial for both attraction and connection.

YOU CAN STILL BE A BADASS

My client Craig ("Mr. Clutch" from Chapter 5), forty-seven, is a divorced father of two who's into football and rock climbing. Guy stuff. He started dating Karen, a thirty-eight-year-old investor. She invited him to a party at her family's lake house. "He disappeared and I found him in the kids' playroom," Karen told me. "He was sitting at a tiny pink table with my four-year-old niece and her giant teddy bear. They were all wearing pink bows in their hair—the teddy bear, too—and having a tea party with pink cups. I just melted. I said to myself, 'That's my future husband.'"

Nothing is manlier to women than not caring how manly you look. Empathy and kindness are not emasculating. On the contrary: It's about the manliest thing you can do.

As writer Page Turner explained on Bolde.com, "There's nothing sexier than a man in touch with his feminine side and I'm never going back to dating guys who aren't." The reasons she cited include "they let you know they care," they are better communicators, and they know that sometimes the hottest thing you can say to a woman is "I'm sorry." Added Turner, "Forget the strong silent type. There's nothing sexier than a man who can apologize when he's wrong."[7]

A guy can be a bit feminine and still be a badass. As for cinematic models to follow, you can keep James Bond and Dirty Harry. I'll take "Crash" Davis, Kevin Costner's hard-drinking, tough-talking, minor-league catcher in *Bull Durham*. He's plenty manly. But he also reads Susan Sontag novels and paints his lady's toenails in the tub. And when he tells Susan Sarandon's character that he believes in "long, slow, deep, soft, wet kisses that last three days," she pants, "*Oh myyy*."

True, in dating, you generally want to lead with masculinity, but the longer you talk to a woman, the more your softer, lovey-dovey side can show. You become a sheep in wolf's clothing.

Do this not only for a better dating life. Do it for yourself, so you can grow into the superior guy Hemingway reached for but failed to become. "You're creating soil, rich soil, for you and your growth," writes John Kim in the book *I Used to Be a Miserable F*ck*. "You're raising your potential. You're positioning yourself. You're building a better, stronger you."[8]

ESCAPE THE "MAN BOX"

Building a better you can be challenging if you were raised to be tough and stoic, writes Lewis Howes in *The Mask of Masculinity*. "The problem is when that toughness doesn't stop and it grows like cancer until it strangles all other feelings."[9]

This happens because masculinity has traditionally been defined in an overly narrow way. Be macho. Take risks. Don't act girly. Fear weakness.

Don't be like women—objectify them. In his TED Talk, activist Tony Porter calls it the "man box." He echoes what author bell hooks writes in *All About Love*: "Patriarchal masculinity estranges men from their selfhood."[10]

Social scientists have noted for decades that our old conception of masculinity contributes to a lowered life expectancy, tension-related disease, and a suicide rate in men that's more than triple that of women. The patriarchy pulverizes everyone.

Break out of that box. Embracing your feminine side is good for your love life, good for women, and good for the world. It will make you a better dater, a better boyfriend, a better husband, a better dad, and a better person.

CHAPTER 6 MISSIONS

Two Steps to Letting Women See Your Softer Side

1. **Work on Developing Your Sense of Empathy**
   Channeling the feminine self is largely about empathy—first being in touch with what you feel, and then with what others feel. To cultivate empathy, ask a date, friend, or family member how they're feeling about something that's important to them. Then, don't problem-solve. Just listen. This is great practice for your upcoming dates and for your future girlfriend. When a woman vents after a tough day, more often than not she doesn't want a fix. She wants a sympathetic ear.

2. **Show Vulnerability with a Story**
   On your next date or interaction with a woman, look for the right moment to share a true, vulnerable story—one that reveals a flaw or fear, or maybe just something you royally screwed up. For example, I might talk about my wife leaving me nine weeks after our wedding, or the day I walked into my boss's office expecting a big promotion—and got canned instead.

SO WHAT HAVE WE LEARNED?

....

- Women are drawn to your masculine essence as well as to your feminine side. They want to see both selves.
- Reject the "man box." A man can be strong and masculine as well as vulnerable and in touch with his softer side.
- What do you want from me? That Joe Pesci can act!
- You contain multitudes, and they're all enough.

IT'S NOT YOU—
IT'S THE HALIBUT
YOU'RE HOLDING

HOW TO GET GOOD
AT ONLINE DATING

You don't suck. Your profile sucks.
Fix your profile and you fix your online-dating problems.
—Connell Barrett; dating coach, author, narcissistic self-quoter

....

She had a face to launch a thousand swipes.

Veronica was beautiful, well read, and our phone banter was as snappy as Hepburn-Tracy dialogue. She just might be "The One," I told myself. I'd flown three thousand miles to surprise her, and she would call any minute now. Yep, any minute.

We'd connected online but hadn't yet met in person—she lived in San Francisco, I lived in New York. But judging by our chemistry, we were surely about to begin an epic love affair. And when she got the goods I left on her front steps (a dozen red roses, a lacy Victoria's Secret number, and a note telling her I was in town) she'd for sure be mine. Right?

Wrong. She ghosted me. I was devastated.

Looking back at it now, however, I realize that she was totally right to blow me off. By flying cross-country, I'd tripped her Desperate Guy alarm. That's what a scarcity of dating options can make a guy do. At the time, I didn't have a single good romantic option in New York, so I flew all the way to California to make a grand, eighties rom com–level gesture. I put so much pressure on Veronica that she had no choice but to disappear.

I didn't realize all of that at the time. I was just hurt and confused. But hitting bottom can be a good thing. As Chuck Palahniuk writes in the novel *Fight Club*, "It's only after you've lost everything that you're free to do anything."[1]

After Veronica, I was determined to do whatever it took to become great at online dating. I studied with the top experts and tested dozens of different profiles, learning what works on Tinder, Bumble, Match, or any dating app. After a lot of trial and error, I finally figured out the truth about online-dating success, and everything changed. Using the same tools I'm about to teach you, I once matched with over two hundred attractive women on Tinder in a single week. Feeling ambitious over one four-day weekend, I went on seven dates—and five of them were into me. That kind of abundance feels incredible.

Along the way, I realized something simple but powerful. Online dating isn't really "dating." It's marketing. You're basically just running a digital ad for yourself. (You may have negative associations with the idea of marketing, but it can be done with integrity. More on that in a minute.)

In this chapter, we're going to overhaul your online-dating profile, turning Tinder, Bumble, Hinge, The League, or any app from a black hole of frustration into a funnel of single women for you to message and to date. I'll share my five rules for online-dating success, which include a crash course in how to text women. What's great is that once you get your profile dialed in, you can "set it and forget it"—that is, just swipe a few days a week, get *lots* of quality matches, and then meet the women you're most interested in dating. This gives you lots of options and lots of confidence.

PLENTY OF FISH PHOTOS

You need a damn good dating profile because the online-dating competition is stiff. According to a study by the research firm GlobalWebIndex, 62 percent of all location-based dating-app users are male.[2] On Tinder, the most popular app in the world, men outnumber women by a four-to-one margin, and a UK study by mobile-data specialist Ogury put the number at a whopping nine-to-one.[3]

With so much choice, it's no wonder that women only swipe right about 14 percent of the time on Tinder, while men swipe right at a 46 percent clip, according to the *New York Times*.[4] A similar scenario plays out on Bumble and Plenty of Fish, the second and third most-used apps, respectively. These daunting odds make it difficult for the typical guy to get matches and messages when he's swiping for love. And it helps explain why about six out of ten men who try online dating report receiving too little interest from women, according to the Pew Research Center, while only one in four women say they get too little interest from men.[5]

If you're like most guys, you either get very few (if any) matches and dates, or you don't match with the kinds of women you want. (If you've never used Tinder or a swiping app, a match is when both you and a woman "like" each other's profile, freeing you to start messaging one another.)

The likely cause of your disappointing results? Again, online dating is really just marketing, and your marketing campaign is hurting you. Perhaps your photos are dark and grainy, or there are group shots that make it hard to tell which guy is you . . . and what's up with the shot of you holding that fish? (She doesn't want to date Quint from *Jaws*.)

Online dating doesn't suck. Your profile sucks. In other words, it's not you. It's the halibut you're holding. This is great news because you wouldn't be able to "fix" online dating. But you *can* fix your marketing.

SLEAZY COME, SLEAZY GO
....

The very concept of "marketing" probably makes you think of sleazy, deceitful, used-car-salesmen tactics. But done with integrity, the right marketing message creates genuine trust with an audience. In the 1960s, the Avis car-rental company admitted its second-tier status to Hertz with the slogan, "We're No. 2 so we try harder." The result of such refreshing honesty? Avis nearly doubled its market share. More recently, Southwest Airlines promised fliers "Transfarency," meaning no hidden fees. The campaign racked up nearly 5 million Facebook "likes."

You want to market yourself to women in a similar way—with integrity and authenticity. This not only feels great. It's also what works.

As with any piece of good marketing, your dating profile must do three things:

1. It must be **disruptive**, meaning it stands out and snaps women out of their "swiping hypnosis."

2. It must be **valuable**. There's something in it for her—a date, a fling, a great relationship. In other words, a clear upside.

3. It must create **trust**. If a woman can't trust you, she won't date you.

That's the essence of marketing done right: disrupt, offer value, and create trust and connection.

DON'T BELIEVE THE SWIPE!

You may think that women use dating apps the same way that men do, but that's not the case. When swiping on Tinder, us guys follow this complex psychological algorithm:

Whoa, she's hot! [Swipe right]

Sure, we want smart, kind women with inner beauty, but men are visual beings. We swipe for looks first and ask questions later.

However, women don't use Tinder and other apps that way. They filter guys out using a three-part screening process. Ladies swipe left as quickly as gents do, but it takes the typical woman ten times longer to swipe right, according to Tinder's own research.[6] They have to be more discerning because they have so many options. In addition, women tend to focus more on the emotions and personality conveyed by your photos, rather than solely on looks.

Here's what must happen for a woman to match with you on Tinder.

1. **She looks at your featured photo and says yes or no**
   If your main picture blends in with all the other guys she sees, it doesn't register with her, and she swipes left. If your lead

photo engages her, she'll be interested—but probably not sold yet. Next . . .

2. **She reads your bio and says yes or no**
   If what you wrote bores or confuses her, or she sees a red flag (say, a vulgar comment), then you're done. But if your bio has personality and charm . . .

3. **She views the rest of your photos and *then* swipes left or right**
   If your other pictures speak to her, with no deal-breaking shots (such as your appearing drunk or holding a fish . . . or holding a fish while drunk), she finally swipes right.
   Your looks are a fairly minor factor. She swipes based on how your photos make her feel, not where you fall on a 1 to 10 scale.

A heads-up. I talk a lot about Tinder, because it's the granddaddy of dating apps with the biggest user base—50 million worldwide members swiping a billion times daily. But these concepts apply to most of the top dating sites. And don't let its rep as the hookup app dissuade you. Sure, Tinder has facilitated more one-night stands than Cuervo Gold, but it's also a good option for finding a serious connection—maybe even better than IRL dating. A study commissioned by the app found that its users are more likely than offline daters to be seeking a committed relationship, according to the *New York Times*.[7]

Let's go deeper and discuss the five fundamentals that get you more matches and dates.

FIRST RULE OF ONLINE-DATING SUCCESS: POST MAGNETIC PHOTOS

With the right photos, you're 75 percent of the way to success. With the wrong photos, you can swipe and swipe and get nothing but carpal tunnel.

Most men tend to slap together a few random pictures without applying any strategy. But again, online dating is a form of advertising. As Don Draper says in *Mad Men*, "Advertising is based on one thing: happiness."[8] Your photos must make women feel happy about what dating you might be like.

Although your profile features you, it's not *about* you. It's about her. It's about giving a potential hot date those warm fuzzies. Think of your pictures as a curated photo essay titled "Meet Your Dream Dude."

PARDON THE INTERRUPTION

Your featured photo is the most important piece of real estate on your profile. If your lead photo is weak, you can end up in the Tinder hinterland, with few or zero good matches. The featured picture is the first image women see, so you must hook them fast, or else they'll swipe left.

The photo that kicks off your profile should be a "pattern interrupter." On Tinder and most dating apps, women fall into a kind of swiping hypnosis, seeing the same sorts of shots over and over: shirtless selfies, backward caps, fishing pics aplenty. You must disrupt their pattern to capture their attention. To do that, make your featured photo a high-quality portrait, showing you at your most attractive, dateable self.

This is a game changer. Nothing works better than a magnetic portrait.

The image should be crisp, clear, and bright, ideally shot with natural light, which tends to be more flattering than artificial light. You'll want to zoom in close and shoot from the waist or chest up. Look at the lens—eye contact increases the sense of connection with the audience. (That said, experiment with angular shots, since they can work well if you have a strong jawline.) And smile—a *real* smile, not a fake, forced smile. (Leave the smoldering glares to Zoolander.) Dress first-date great. No sweats, no ball caps, no cargo shorts—no exceptions.

Here's an example of what *not* to do: I'm smirking (not smiling), my face is in shadow, and the sky and water draw as much focus as I do. When I tested this photo on my Tinder account, my match rate plummeted.

Upgrading your featured photo can have dramatic results even without any other profile tweaks. My client Kevin (Higher Self name: "King Kong")—an attractive, eligible, divorced health-care worker in his forties—was struggling to get matches. The problem? His first photo was a shadowy, grim-faced selfie that he'd snapped in his garage. (He looked like Dexter in his kill room.) Kevin upgraded to a handsome, sunny outdoor shot, showcasing a big smile and a pressed, powder-blue button-down. Within a day, he had fourteen matches that he was psyched about.

SHOOT TO THRILL

Your first photo is pivotal, but you'll also want a second quality portrait to help you seal the deal—one that has a different vibe than the first shot. I recommend you do a photo shoot with a professional photographer. (Try googling "online-dating photog-

SWIPE LEFT! This photo of me tanked on Tinder because women see countless low-quality selfies, the light is unflattering, and I'm not smiling.

raphers" or "social media photographers" in your area. You can also use a friend who's good with a camera.) Bring at least two different outfits and shoot at a couple different locations—say, in a park and also in your home. Take *lots* of shots. (Most will not be usable.) Your goal is to end up with five to ten excellent portraits.

A *very* important photo-shoot tip: Put yourself in a loose, fun emotional state, so that you're literally laughing and cracking jokes while your photographer is snapping away. (When she's shooting me, my photographer Riane makes faces and curses like a Teamster because she knows it makes me laugh.) Why should you do this? Because authentic, natural smiles are much more attractive to women than forced smiles. A real smile—one born from true joy—activates your orbicularis oculi, the circular muscle that surrounds each eye. When you fake a grin, it looks, well, fake because you can't independently move those eye muscles. But when genuine emotions spark a smile, those eye muscles activate, your eyes twinkle, and your whole face lights up—and it gives women that happy feeling. (Google "Duchenne smile" to learn more about this.)

I've split-tested my clients' portraits on Photofeeler—a site that offers focus-group feedback on dating-app pictures—and women rate real smiles as 25 to 50 percent more attractive than stiff, "say cheese" smiles. That means more matches and dates. So make sure your smile is authentic, almost like you didn't know you would be photographed. Women love that candid, real, caught-in-the-moment vibe.

After your photo shoot, take five to ten of your best portraits and test them on Photofeeler, to get unbiased feedback from women. You can also ask female friends to pick their favorites. You'll want to take your top-scoring portrait and make that your featured dating-app photo. In the second slot, use the highest-rated portrait that has a different look *and* a different outfit from your featured photo.

Congrats! You'll now have two magnetic, handsome portraits for the top two spots on your profile. The most important part is handled.

"AWW" YEAH!

For the picture to go in the third slot, I recommend what I call an "Aww" photo—one that tugs on the heartstrings and makes women go, "Aww." It could be you with your dog or playing with your little nephew (get the parents' permission before using) or dancing with your grandma. My "Aww" photo shows me and my niece at her wedding, featuring me in "loving uncle" mode.

So now you've got a strong 1-2-3 punch. Your first two, focus group-tested photos show you at your most attractive and dateable, and the third shot conveys real heart. Your photo essay is looking like this.

Photo 1: An attractive portrait, with you well dressed, smiling a real smile, and (probably) looking at the camera.

Photo 2: Another high-quality portrait, but with a different outfit and back-drop, giving her a sense of variety.

Photo 3: Your "Aww" photo. Tug at those heart-strings. (My niece Tarah and me. How flippin' cute are we? Notice how I write "My Niece" on the photo so

SWIPE RIGHT! This is as handsome as I get without Botox. The light flatters me, and I look first-date great, complete with leather jacket.

that women know Tarah's not my date or an ex.)

As a woman swipes through these first three shots, I want her feeling: [first photo] *Cute and dateable* . . . [next photo] *Ooh, nice style* . . . [next photo] *Aww! Loving uncle! Right-swipe!* (Yes, a very strong 1-2-3 punch can yield a match before she even reads your bio.)

A total of six to nine photos is the sweet spot. (Too few won't give her a big enough window into your life and personality. Too many can make you come across as narcissistic.) For the photos that follow your first three, favor shots that showcase your passions—running a marathon, playing guitar, cooking, tearing up the dance floor. Other great options include you in Social Guy mode—say, at a classy lounge with friends. And anything edgy (you in a cool leather jacket) or adventuresome (climbing a rock wall, skydiving, or hiking) is a great option, especially if you have a nice-guy vibe. (Girls like a little edge.) And if you have another good portrait, feel free to put that in the last slot.

A great, stylish portrait.

My niece and me. Aww!

Your final order will go something like this: 1) Awesome portrait. 2) Awesome portrait with a different vibe/clothes. 3) "Aww" photo. 4) Cool hobby. 5) Social Guy. 6) Rock-wall climbing. 7) A different awesome portrait.

Here are some shots you *don't* want to include:

- You shirtless, unless you're at the beach. And even then, you need the pecs and abs to pull it off.
- Selfies. They're common, and depending on the angle, can give you seven chins.

- Group shots. If she has to work hard to decipher which one is you, she'll swipe left.
- You wearing sunglasses, which breaks the eye contact and connection you want.
- Fish photos.
- You doing a polarizing activity, say, hunting or smoking.
- Ball caps.
- You in shorts. Unless you're in the Tour de France, cover your legs. The female form is like Botticelli's *The Birth of Venus*. Us guys? More like *Dogs Playing Poker*.

SECOND RULE OF ONLINE-DATING SUCCESS: WRITE A BADASS BIO

Most dating-app bios suffer from a fatal case of I-Like-Long-Walks-on-the-Beach-itis. They're dull and they read like a résumé. Here are the key elements you want in your bio:

- Clarity. Women want to burn minimal mental calories while reading about you. If you confuse, she will snooze, and you will lose.
- Personality! It should be light, fun, and authentic. Humor is a major bonus. Making her laugh is better than having six-pack abs.
- Positivity. Good vibes only.
- Brevity. Less is more.
- Sincerity and heart. Let her glimpse the real you, with specifics.
- Some "chick bait," that is, stuff that women are drawn to: dogs, yoga, the beach, surfing, a cool job, delicious foods such as guacamole. (A study by the dating app Zoosk noted that men who mention guac on their profile saw their match rate increase by 144 percent on average.[9])

- A call to action, such as a fun question ("Would you rather date Tyrion or Jon Snow?") or telling her what she should do. ("Swipe right if you love Pop-Tarts.")
- Visual appeal, with line breaks and an emoji or two. (No eggplants! Think winky or laughing smiley faces.) Avoid a dense block of hard-to-read text.

What not to put in your bio:

- Negativity, such as listing what you *don't* want in a partner.
- Any variation of "no drama." Women hate this because it's like saying, "Have no emotions and be perfect."
- Vulgarity.
- *Nothing*. No blank bios. Write something.
- Fat-shaming, slut-shaming, bi-shaming, and STI-shaming (e.g., referring to yourself as "clean"). This won't work, it's gross, and may get your profile banned.

BE CAPTAIN "HOOK"

Just as your featured photo is the most important image on your profile, the first sentence is the most important part of your bio. I call it the hook. If your first line doesn't hook her interest, she may bounce.

Things to avoid are clichés, like "giving this a try" (duh!) and "seeking a partner in crime" (don't use, unless you're a bank robber). Generic greetings like "Whattup, ladies?" will fall flat. Another turn-off? Writing "I'm bad at bios." Would you buy an iPhone if Apple's slogan was "We're bad at technology"? And no quoting your favorite movie or TV show. (Great, you like *The Office*—most of humanity does.)

As of this writing, on Tinder your hook appears as a caption on your featured photo, so if you nail both the opening portrait and the hook, you can see a big spike in matches.

The best way to grab her attention is with a good quip. Make her smile. This is more art than science, so here are some examples my clients and I have had success with.

"DANGER! My profile *may* make you fall in love with me."
Why it works: The all-caps breaks her pattern, and the "challenge" issued creates curiosity. You're daring her NOT to keep reading.

"A man on the street and a dad bod in the sheets."
Why it works: Even if she doesn't know the Usher song lyric that this alludes to, it's silly and self-effacing. Most guys brag on Tinder. You're talking up your dad bod.

"I'm 6'2", so I'm the perfect big spoon."
Why it works: It combines two things women love: tall guys and spooning.

"My million-dollar idea: Pulled. Pork. Ice cream."
Why it works: Just plain stupid, in the best way. If she laughs, she'll keep reading.

"My heart is bigger than Kanye's ego."
Why it works: A snarky dig at Kanye while saying, *I'm a good guy*. That's an attractive combo.

"Back in my day, we made booty calls on pay phones."
Why it works: A funny way to tweak Tinder.

How to Write about Yourself
Include a few details in your bio about you. What do you want women to know? What makes you different, awesome, a great catch? Show (with specifics), don't tell (with vagueness). "I live for rock climbing in Colorado" paints a clear picture. "I love to travel" or "I like the outdoors" says nothing.

How to Write a Good Call to Action

End your bio with a fun call to action that compels her to match with you. This is especially important on Bumble, where women send the first message; you're helping her write her opener to you. "Would you rather" questions work well because they're playful and easy to answer. Such as, WYR . . .

- . . . have dinner with Lennon or McCartney?
- . . . shower in Evian or swim in Cristal?
- . . . date the Tin Man or Scarecrow?
- . . . eat a potato, or BE a potato?

Calls to action can simply tell her what you want her to do, the same way we're all told to "Call now!" or "Like and subscribe." The secret? Make her want to swipe.

- "Swipe right if you love Ben & Jerry's."
- "Swipe right if you're too sexy for this app."
- "What kind of puppy should I get? Message me!"
- "Tell me . . . Thin-crust or deep-dish? (Pressure. There IS a right answer.)"

PUTTING IT ALL TOGETHER

This four-line approach to writing your bio works well. I'll use my own profile as a model.

Line 1: The hook makes her smile. *DANGER! My karaoke voice will make you swoon.*

Line 2: List some cool stuff about you, and mention your career and/or family to show some heart. If possible, inject humor. *Loves: my job as a dating coach, my 5 fabulous siblings, red wine, trips to Italy, and jaywalking. (Yeah, I'm a bad boy.)*

Line 3: Say what you're looking for in a woman, and/or what your first date might be. *If you're smart, silly, and love big books, let's get 2 glasses of red.*

Line 4: Call her to action. *I'm puppy-shopping. Should I get . . . a Frenchie or an English bulldog?*

And just like that, poof! Finished bio, in fifty-nine lean, mean words. (Make sure you include a couple emojis as well.)

> **DANGER! My karaoke voice will make you swoon.**
>
> **Loves: My job as a dating coach, my 5 fabulous siblings, red wine, trips to Italy, and jaywalking. (Yeah, I'm a bad boy.)**
>
> **If you're smart, silly, and love big books, let's get 2 glasses of red.**
>
> **I'm puppy-shopping. Should I get . . . a Frenchie or an English bulldog?**

There's no one-size-fits-all bio formula; many approaches can work. Here are three more of mine that I like.

The Listicle: A fun list is hard to resist. Notice how I talk directly to her, convey my sense of humor, and throw in lots of "chick bait."

> **4 TRUE THINGS ABOUT ME**
>
> **1: I can seductively whisper Italian in your ear.**
> **2: My homemade guac will make you 😋**
> **3: I'm a dating coach . . . like Hitch! (Seriously.)**
> **4: I like big books and I cannot lie . . .**
> **What's a true thing about you?**

The Rave Review: Steal the trick that movie trailers use. Don't worry about quote accuracy. Just go for laughs.

> **The reviews are in!**
>
> **"Connell is very handsome."** —My mom
>
> **"I wish I had his muscles."** —The Hulk
>
> **"Just so you know, he used to sleep with a stuffed pig."**
> —My big sister
>
> **OK, what do people say about you?**

The Costanza: This approach is inspired by a *Seinfeld* episode[10] in which George Costanza realizes that brutal honesty works better with women than lying does. Write something totally honest that doesn't make you look "cool." (But no oversharing and nothing overtly sexual.) Many women find this refreshing and funny. Keep them short. Here are three I've written for clients.

- *I'm chubby and not rich, but I have a job, a car, and I'll never send you a dick pic.*
- *That's not really my dog. I just want to match with you.*
- *I like women with incredible bodies. If you like my abs, let's meet up.*

Test different bios until the matches start to pour in. As long as it represents your best, most authentic self—in a way that engages her—you can't go wrong.

THIRD RULE OF ONLINE-DATING SUCCESS: WRITE COMPELLING OPENERS

So, you started getting matches. Huzzah! Now the fun part. Flirting, chatting, and connecting! And that all starts with a good opener.

First, what *not* to do: Don't begin with "Hey" or "How's your day?" or "What's up?" or any other variation of "Hello." It bores women and shows them that you made no effort. Starting with "Hey" is akin to saying, "Hey, will you ignore this message and un-match me?" Remember, she likely has lots of guys messaging her, so you have to stand out.

The best openers have three things in common.

- They're personalized to her, showing that you read her bio.
- They're light, playful, and friendly. They may be flirty but not overtly sexual.
- They're not too short or too long. One to three sentences is about right.

Here are some fun, effective ways to write your openers.

THE COMPLIMENT + QUESTION

Look at her bio and see what strikes you as quirky, interesting, or cool—say, her style, her love for hiking, her fondness for Steve Carell. Tell her what impressed you, and ask her a question that she would enjoy answering. A great way to frame your opener is making her an expert. (We all love being experts.) Use her name, and limit yourself to two emojis.

"Katie . . . I see you're a Steve Carell fan. Awesome. OK, lemme ask you. Do you think he's better in comedies or dramas?"

You're making her an expert in a topic she likes, while also showing that you read her bio. She's likely to reply.

COMPLIMENT + TEASE

You pay a sincere, specific compliment—but instead of asking a question, you tease her about something, such as her favorite TV shows or a silly accessory she's wearing in a shot. (*Never* tease about anything she would likely take offense at, such as her appearance, or anything that's too personal.) Let's say her bio mentions traveling in Europe, and in one shot she's wearing a bold, colorful hat.

"Katie, wow! You've backpacked all over Europe? I'm impressed. But I'm curious . . . did the fashion police in Italy arrest you for that hat?"

A compliment paired with a tease can entice her to spar with you.

CLEVER ICEBREAKERS

I much prefer personalized openers, but here are five one-size-fits-all icebreakers that also work well. (Make sure to include the woman's name so it feels more specific to her.)

- "So, how does this online-dating thing work? Are we, like, engaged now?"
- "Whattaya think? Should we exchange small talk for 3 weeks & then never meet?"
- "I know this is a fake profile and you're probably a dude, but can you get me the name of the model you used for your pic?"
- "How do I get laid on Tinder?" Then, your second text: "Oh, shit! This isn't Google . . ."
- "Stop looking so damn, distractingly cute. I'm trying to get some work done."

Final notes about openers:

- Avoid being too sexual too soon, such as commenting on her body parts or talking about sexual acts. That said . . .
- Be Man-to-Woman. Let her know she's attractive, but in a PG-rated way. You might open with, "Damn! That photo of you on the beach melted my iPhone." Also, play around with innuendo. A client matched with a curvaceous attorney, and the opener I wrote for him

was, "Counselor, you have a rebuttal that just won't quit." Cleverness is not required, but it does help.

- If she doesn't reply to the opener after a couple days, don't give up yet. She may be busy or not using the app. Follow up with a second message, treating it almost like a P.S. to your first. This makes her think to herself, *Oh, right! I need to reply to that cool guy I matched with.* She may appreciate your persistence and charm. Never, ever say anything like, "Hey, did you get my message?" or "Why haven't you written back?"

Your openers don't have to be Shakespearean. Just light and fun, and (usually) about her. And the better your entire profile is, the more interested in you she will become—and the less amazing your openers need to be.

And when your profile is totally dialed in, awesome things happen. A couple of times a week on Bumble or Tinder, a woman I match with will send me an opener, something like: "Hey, Connell! I love your profile. We should meet up. My number is 917 . . ."

When women give you their numbers out of the gate—those are the best openers of all.

FOURTH RULE OF ONLINE-DATING SUCCESS: KNOW HOW TO TEXT AND MESSAGE WOMEN

In the Digital Age, texting has never been more important to dating results. Here's my simple texting philosophy in four words:

Give, Give, Give, Ask.

Most of your messages should give her something of value: jokes, compliments, teases, cat memes, song lyrics, thought-provoking questions, or more often than anything, just sincere, authentic conversation. Then, every so often, you ask for what you want: her number or a date. When you give a lot, a woman is much more likely to say yes when you ask for something. She will *want* to give back because she's looking for a guy who makes her feel good and brings value to her life.

But too many guys text the opposite way. They ask, ask, ask—and then ask some more. They ask boring questions. ("How's your day?") They ask for dates way too soon. They ask for validation. All of this gets them nowhere. Because to get, you have to give.

Here's a texting lesson on what *not* to do. I'll call this client Barry, who had a good first date with Rachel, and then . . . ouch. She went from liking him to ghosting him, because all he did was ask, rather than give.

> BARRY [12:03 a.m. Mon]: I'm home. Hope you had as good of a time as I did and that we can go out again soon.

> RACHEL [12:04 a.m. Mon]: I did have a great time! I hope we do :)

> BARRY [12:04 a.m. Mon]: I'm looking forward to it. When is the next day you don't have to get up early for anything?

> BARRY [9:07 p.m. Mon]: How was your day?

> BARRY [10:20 a.m. Tues]: Come hang out with me.

> BARRY [3:46 p.m. Tues]: Did you drop the class or just give up on coming?

> BARRY [10:39 p.m. Wed]: Good morning.

Barry's big mistake? He immediately went into "ask" mode *less than a minute* after she said good night. He "asked" three more times in the next two days, while also being boring. ("How was your day?") It's no surprise that Rachel turned into Casper.

If you get stuck on how to give, ask yourself, *What could I write that would make her smile?*

(To see my texting philosophy in action, see my text exchange with Annie in the previous chapter.)

FIFTH RULE OF ONLINE-DATING SUCCESS: KNOW WHEN AND HOW TO ASK HER OUT

The typical guy waits too long to ask for a woman's number, so she either gets bored, or thinks he's too afraid to take a chance. Here are some important guidelines about asking for her number/asking her out.

- Before you go for her number, plan to discuss one or two topics with her (three at most) over the course of a dozen or so messages. That said, if a woman is upbeat right away, you can go for her number after just one topic and a few messages.
- Once you've exhausted two or three topics, *definitely* go for it. She wants a date, not a pen pal. The sooner the two of you take things off of Tinder, the better. When you graduate to texting, you're elevated in her mind above all the other guys she's matched with. Get off the app A and SAP!
- Should you *only* ask for her number, or should you ask her out and then take her number? Either can work. I prefer the former because it's simple and efficient. Get the digits while on the app, and sort out the details later by text.

Here's a simple, classy way to ask for her number. "Hey, [name], you seem [something you like about her]. We should text off the app. What's your number?"

Another great time to ask is immediately after you've made her laugh and she "LOL"s you. She's in a receptive mood, so take action. Message something like, "You have a great sense of humor. Let's text off the app. What's your number?"

Here's a text to send after she laughs at something you wrote: "So, how funny was that, on a scale of (000)-000-0000 to (999)-999-9999?"

Once you get her number, text her sooner rather than later. In fact, you can message her right away. No, this is not needy—as long as you follow the texting philosophy of Give, Give, Give, Ask. Keep the good vibes going and set up a first date over text.

Important: The clock is ticking! In general, after you get her number, you have between three and seven days to get her out on a date before the trail goes cold. The longer you put it off, the less likely it is you'll meet up with her.

OTHER BURNING
ONLINE-DATING QUESTIONS

SHOULD I GO FOR PREMIUM MEMBERSHIPS, SUCH AS TINDER GOLD?

Yes. Top-tier memberships assure that the maximum number of women see your profile—all for the monthly price of a mojito, on most apps. That's a bargain.

Now, you may be saying, "But Tinder Gold has never worked for me." That's your profile's fault, not the app's. Any dating app can work for you with the right photos and bio. Tinder Gold won't magically make a poor profile attractive. But with the right profile, it definitely delivers results, as do the premium versions of Bumble, Hinge, Coffee Meets Bagel, and The League.

While you may be tempted to watch your wallet, don't scrimp here. You get what you pay for with dating apps.

SHOULD I "BOOST" MY PROFILE?

Yes. Boosting is very valuable, no matter what app you use. When you boost, your profile goes to the front of the line, and the maximum number of women see you. In fact, the first thing you should do after upgrading your profile is go on Tinder Gold during "prime time," between 7 p.m. and 10 p.m., Sunday through Thursday, and do a thirty-minute boost, while also swiping during that time.

This is when you learn how effective your new profile really is. You'll either get quality matches and likes, or you won't. If awesome matches start rolling in, high-five! If you don't see noticeable results on Tinder Gold, then there's still work to be done.

WHAT IF I BOOST AND GET POOR RESULTS?

Panic not. Repeat after me: "Bring the data, not the drama."

This is a marketing mantra to help you focus on the numbers—and potential solutions—rather than going to a bad emotional place.

A lack of matches does NOT mean you're unattractive. It merely means that your marketing needs work.

Many times I've launched my dating profile and gotten poor *initial* results. But I improve it every time. How? By fiddling with and testing different photos and versions of my bio. This is what digital marketers do, and it's what you may have to do.

So, if you launch a new profile and you get tons of matches, you party. If you don't, you ponder. Revisit your featured photo, and the rest of your pics, and look for a potential weak link. (Lack of matches on any app is usually related to photos.) Reread your bio. Any red flags? Anything that might be turning women off?

Sometimes a small change, such as slotting in a new featured photo, can create a big improvement. Bio tweaks can help, too. When my client Randy ("The Czar") launched his Tinder profile, he had really good photos, but his match results were meh. We realized his bio was a bit bland and too "nice guy." We swapped in one photo of him in a black leather jacket, and we changed his hook, that all-important first line, to this: "If you can handle a man who's a little cocky, we might get along." He doubled his matches, and women were soon messaging him, saying, "So, what makes YOU so cocky? ;)"

You can do this! It just takes trial and error.

Bring the data, not the drama.

SHOULD I USE SUPER LIKES?

Yes. Use any feature that assures women see your profile. On Tinder, a Super Like notifies her that you're interested, putting your profile at the top of her queue. The more women who see you, the better your chances for matches—again, with a well-curated profile.

SHOULD I USE THE VIDEO LOOP FEATURE?

Definitely. From Tinder to Hinge to The League, the top apps are letting users post short video clips on their profiles. Video brings you to life, so I recommend it. In the clip, be doing something physical (water-skiing, shooting hoops), fun (making a face, dancing), or adorable (I have a puppy licking my face).

HOW MANY MATCHES SHOULD I EXPECT WHEN MY PROFILE IS HUMMING?

It depends on which app you're using and where you live. But if you're based in a major metro area, you could easily be looking at five to ten matches a day (out of a hundred right-swipes), for up to thirty-five to seventy matches a week. Those kinds of numbers make it easy to get a couple of dates per week.

I'VE HEARD ABOUT TINDER'S RATING SYSTEM. IS THERE ANYTHING I SHOULD KNOW ABOUT IT?

Most apps, such as Tinder, use an algorithm that assigns an internal score that essentially rates your profile's effectiveness, based on factors such as how many women match with you, the quality of those matches, and how often you swipe. Basically, the more "attractive" and relevant your profile is, the higher your score—and the more frequently your profile gets shown to women who have good ratings.

Don't stress too much about your score on Tinder, especially since you'll never know what it is! If you have a good profile, your score and your matches will take care of themselves. Just avoid behaviors that can hurt your internal rating, like right-swiping on *everyone*, and matching with women but not messaging them. (Tinder doesn't like that.)

I don't worry about my score *at all*, thanks to the boosting feature. If my score degrades, I simply do a boost in prime time. When your profile is boosted, Tinder essentially gives you a perfect rating during that period, meaning that the most desirable women get to see you. With great pics and a killer bio, you'll get all the matches and dates you need while also repairing your score nice and high. Now that's abundance.

CHAPTER 7 MISSIONS

Five Steps to Getting Matches and Dates on the Dating App of Your Choice

1. **Take and Test New Photos**
   Using the concepts from this chapter, storyboard and execute a photo shoot that results in five to ten new portraits. Then, before posting on the dating app of your choice, test the strongest selections on Photofeeler, the site that offers focus-group feedback on dating photos.

2. **Write Your Profile Bio**
   Use the four-line formula I provided, personalizing it for you.

3. **Practice Crafting Openers**
   Find the profiles of five women you find attractive and, whether or not you've matched with them, write three practice openers for each profile. That's fifteen openers total. (If you did match with any of them, send your favorite opener to her.)

4. **Compliment Five More Women**
   This time, after delivering the compliment, change the subject and try to reach the two-minute mark in each conversation.

5. **Keep Doing Your Confidence Kickoff**
   A reminder: Do your Confidence Kickoff every day. Don't be slacking off, now. Those fifteen minutes each morning will change the game. The way you start your day sets the tone for the rest of your week, year, and life.

SO WHAT HAVE WE LEARNED?

....

- Online dating isn't really dating. It's digital marketing.
- With the right collection of portraits, photos, and a great bio, you can get matches and dates on Tinder or any dating app.
- Be ready to make adjustments to your profile. Try different photo and bio combinations until you can "set it and forget it" as the matches roll in.
- After you've matched, get her off the app sooner rather than later.
- The secret to texting: Give, Give, Give, Ask.
- Reason no. 137 that you are enough to date wonderful women: You'll soon have a fantastic dating-app profile that has charm, heart, and is 100 percent fish-free.

⚡ BONUS TIPS ⚡

HOW TO EMOJI
....

Women can emoji till the 🐄s come home, but a man has to find the right balance. Using too many emojis makes him sound like a teenage girl. Not using any makes him a 💩 + 👤 because they work.

Here are six emoji rules to help you find the 🔑 to her 💛.

- End your first text with a 😉. In real life, winking falls somewhere between awkward and restraining order, but in emoji-land it sets a light, flirty tone.

- Use emojis roughly every other text, and max out at two per message—unless she sends you a sexy selfie. Show your appreciation with multiple 😍s.

- Only use 🍆 or 🌋 as a joke, never as a way to get sexual. And smiley faces are just cheesy. The exception? When drenched with irony: "Just found out I need a root canal! 😁"

- Puns pair well with emojis. She wants to grab drinks with you? Don't just say yes—say "Dolphin-itely! 🐬"

- Banish the use of 👅. It won't turn her on. It will make her think of slobber.

- Break any of the above rules after you've hooked up for the first time: 🍆 😍 🌋 👅 🪐 🍑

2030 VISION:
A WORLD WITHOUT BAD DATES

Can you imagine a dating landscape without bad first dates? It's not unthinkable, says one forward-thinker. "My vision is that technology makes dating much more efficient and basically eliminates bad first dates," says Amanda Bradford, founder and CEO of The League, a swiping app that puts a premium on quality of dates over quantity. Bradford foresees virtual reality being the game-changer. "Two people will be able to put on a headset and go on a VR date, even if they're in different cities. Because it's their voices and gestures, they'll get a good sense of their romantic chemistry and whether they want to meet in real life." The upshot? "No more bad first dates. It will all be second dates, with someone you're already into."

CHAPTER 8

YOU HAD ME AT HELLO

GREAT FIRST DATES

> Mitch: Can I—uh—kiss you—goodnight?
> Blanche: Why do you always ask me if you may?
> Mitch: I don't know whether you want me to or not.
> Blanche: Why should you be so doubtful?
> —Tennessee Williams, *A Streetcar Named Desire*[1]

....

I'd been chasing Lisa for nearly a year, and as we sat side by side in a low-lit lounge, we were close to our first kiss. Several months back, she deservedly friend-zoned me after a couple dates, as mentioned in Chapter 1. But we decided to try again.

This night I was much more confident. Since last seeing her, I'd been on dozens of dates, most of which went well. In one stretch, I had three first dates over the course of three nights, all ending in make-outs. I was finally feeling worthy of someone as witty and beautiful as Lisa.

Also, on this second-chance date, the two of us had connected in a deeper way. We'd always had good banter, but now we were bonding on a more emotional level—opening up about past relationships and life-changing trips we'd taken (her to Machu Picchu, me to Ireland and Italy). She looked at me differently now, too. Gone was the overeager dork who had to lie and exaggerate to impress her. She saw a more self-assured man, and she liked what she saw. It was as if we were already a couple.

Still, those first-kiss butterflies are a bitch. Lisa's glossy lips were only inches away, but they may as well have been in Poughkeepsie. So, I gave her a playful test to see if she was ready for lip lockage. I said, "Close your eyes." This telegraphed that I wanted to kiss her. If she closed her eyes, it was a green light. If she didn't, I would still get points for *sort of* trying. Plus, making out would now be on her mind, which would build sexual tension.

"Close my eyes?" she said. "Why?" She smiled. She knew why. She was playing hard to kiss.

"So I can steal your purse," I said.

"You want to kiss me, don't you?"

"Like I'd *ever* kiss you. You have cooties." That made her snort-laugh. "Uh-oh, we have a snorter here," I said. We were clicking better than ever. Although she didn't close her eyes, the spike in good emotions was the window I needed. (A great time to go for the kiss is when your date laughs and leans closer.) I went in, and we made out at long last.

My Lower Self was now in the rearview. Connell Fuckin Barrett was in charge.

Going for the kiss is just one aspect of the all-important first date. The first time you meet a potential partner is a pivotal moment. A great first date can be the gateway to a passionate, loving relationship—and a bad one can make you want to give up on love and join a monastery in Myanmar.

In this chapter, I'll tell you how to plan and structure a first date in a way that boosts your chances for a fun, connected experience. I'll also explain how to dial up romantic chemistry, which makes getting a second date (and a third and a seventh) more likely. And I'll give you tons of practical tips and tools, such as how to ask women out, how to move in for the first kiss, and how to text the next day.

THE TRIANGLE OF CONNECTION
....

A great first date is when two people go from being relative strangers to feeling a strong romantic bond. Here's a visual that shows the arc of an ideal first date. Picture yourself and the woman inside a triangle. And imagine that the triangle consists of three levels. You both begin at the base, on the bottom level and on opposite sides. As time passes, you "escalate" together toward the top, the two of you getting closer and closer.

Here are the three stages of the Triangle of Connection, in chronological order.

"How's the Weather?"

These are the first ten to fifteen minutes of the date. Feel no pressure to be witty or charming here. You can make small talk as you both get comfortable and your nerves settle. Next, you move to . . .

"You and Me"

You'll spend most of the date in this stage, talking primarily about one another, getting more personal as you go. This is where you're Man-to-Woman and connecting on an emotional level. You graduate to . . .

"We"

You and she become "We." You feel like a unit, a couple. (Yes, even on the first meetup.) Ever had a date where you felt like you'd known each other for years? You'd reached the "We" stage.

Natural chemistry does much of the work to get you to "We," but you can help things along by understanding and using the Three Romantic Escalators. They're escalators that help you dial up romantic connection. (Note that these escalators apply not only to the first date but to subsequent dates.)

THE THREE ROMANTIC ESCALATORS

VERBAL/PERSONAL: Ideally, the two of you go from being guarded, polite, or "safe" in what you discuss to being open, vulnerable, and personal. (This can include escalating from G-rated conversation to racier, sexually charged topics.) It's the most important escalator. You *must* get personal, or else you'll stifle romantic connection.

PHYSICAL: You go from being hands-off and not touching to being increasingly physically expressive—say, a hug to start, then playful high fives or taps on the shoulder, followed by hand-holding, kissing, and, sooner or later, sexual intimacy.

LOGISTICAL: This is about changing scenes. You escalate from the first-date venue to another location or two (say, a different bar, or taking a walk) to, eventually, your place or hers. A great date typically has at least one change of scene; otherwise, it can feel stagnant.

Let's go deeper on the Three Romantic Escalators, beginning with Verbal/Personal.

THE ART OF CONNECTION

A great date is not about you saying cool, charismatic lines that make the woman so attracted she fans herself like she's Scarlett O'Hara. You don't need to "attract" her. If she's on a date with you, she already finds you attractive. A great first date is about making an emotional connection. The way to do this is to talk about each other, getting more and more personal as the date progresses. You basically go from "Nice to meet you" to "I've met the *real* you." As you'll learn shortly, you can do this through asking the right questions, playing fun first-date games, and getting more real and vulnerable as the interaction goes on.

I learned a big secret to connecting emotionally when I met Avery, a bright, bubbly SoCal transplant who had just graduated from NYU with a dance degree. We had nothing in common on paper. (I liked *Seinfeld* and self-help books, and she was into Adult Swim and beach reads.) While having "stuff" in common with your date can't hurt, it's more meaningful to have emotional experiences in common. On our first date, Avery and I discovered that our biggest passions (dancing for her, writing for me) made us feel the same way: creative and special. We were already physically attracted to each other, but when we found an emotional commonality, our chemistry redlined. She and I *got* each other. We were a "we."

My client Craig (aka "Mr. Clutch") returned to the singles scene after a rough divorce. He was at the time a forty-five-year-old dad with two young sons and hadn't dated since his twenties. But once he got the hang of making emotional connections, he was soon seeing three women. "And I am *so* not a player," he told me with a laugh. He first connected with Ruby about their shared love of music. It was an intellectual bond with Heather, a reporter for a top newspaper. When he met Karen, he knew she was extra special. "On our first date, we talked for hours about novels and the journey that fiction takes us on," he said of his future girlfriend. "We talked about *All the Light We Cannot See* for an hour. If you find out what touches both of your souls, that's the connection women want."

THREE STEPS TO DEEP CONNECTION

Having commonalities (liking the same movies, music, and cuisines) helps, but when you share emotional experiences, it goes deeper. Here are three steps to creating deep connections on first dates.

1. **Find out what she's passionate about. Ask her, "What lights you up more than anything? What makes you feel fully alive?"**

   SHE MIGHT SAY: "I love to travel, especially Paris—it's my favorite city." She's now given you a "vehicle" she uses for experiencing a powerful emotion. Now, dig a bit deeper.

2. **Identify the underlying emotion. Remember, it's not about Paris. It's about the emotions that Paris kindles in her. To find out what they are, ask, "Why do you love Paris so much?" Maybe she has French ancestry, so Paris connects her to her family. Or perhaps she took cooking classes there, so the underlying feeling is about the joy of growing and learning.**

   SHE MIGHT SAY: "It's just so beautiful. Paris makes me feel like I'm in a movie." That means she prizes feeling special, unique—like a star in a movie.

   This is big! She's just given you the key to connecting with her.

3. **Relate a shared emotional experience from *your* life.**
   When do *you* feel special, unique, like you're starring in a
   movie? Tell her what makes you feel the same way.
   YOU MIGHT SAY: "I totally get how you feel. I feel the same
   way when I hike in the mountains. I feel like I'm in an adventure movie." You've now connected in a deep, authentic way.

There's no need to overthink this. As she describes how she feels about a given passion, you can simply ask yourself, *What makes me feel the same way?* and then share that with her.

LET'S GET PHYSICAL

The second of the three first-date escalators is physical expressiveness, which I also discuss in Chapter 5. Think of physical expressiveness as climbing stairs. You start at the bottom, not the top. If you've ever been that guy who lunges for a good-night kiss—making her feel awkward and you feel creepy—it's because you were at the bottom of the steps and tried to leap to the top. Not good.

BOTTOM STEPS: A warm hug when she arrives, and later a high five or taps on the arm. G-rated stuff. (If she doesn't seem receptive, *you stay at the bottom of the steps.* Always read how she's feeling and adjust accordingly.) If she's liking it, keep climbing.

MIDDLE STEPS: Tossing your arm over her shoulder, whispering in her ear, letting your bodies touch, perhaps brushing her hair from her eyes. I like to "catch" a woman's high five, interlock our fingers, and now we're holding hands.

TOP STEPS: The first kiss, more hand-holding, touching in slightly more personal areas (your hand on her lower back, hers on your torso), nibbling on each other's necks, and eventually petting and sexual intimacy (in private, of course).

These physical expressions need to be paired with congruent verbal escalation. Example: If you're holding hands and whispering in her ear, you'll be saying something personal, sweet, or sexy, not offering her tax advice.

A big benefit of this stair-step approach? It gives your date clarity about how you feel and what you want. If she's not into it, you cease and desist, and thereby not make an awkward kiss attempt that's rebuffed. If she is into it, all the better.

LOCATION, LOCATION, LOCATION

The third romantic escalator is simple and useful, but few men do it mindfully. With logistical escalation, you simply change locations a time or two on your date. Maybe you start off by sitting on a couple of stools at the bar. Then you move to some sofas in a different part of the lounge. A bit later you might say, "I know this awesome late-night spot. Let's get a nightcap." And off you go. We're all wired to want variety. By changing scenes a couple times, you basically give her multiple dates in one night.

Here are some benefits of logistical escalation:

- It makes the date feel like an adventure or journey—an experience other guys are not giving her.
- The date is infused with energy and excitement. Motion is emotion.
- She experiences you in "man-of-action," leadership mode as you guide her from place to place.
- You have more opportunities to be physically expressive as you switch locations (taking her hand, extending a gentlemanly elbow, etc.)
- If you both want to go to your place or to hers at the end of the date, it's easier to do this if you've already been leading her around. A nightcap at your home is just the next stop. (As opposed to spending three hours on the same barstools and then sheepishly saying, "Wanna go back to my place?")

On first dates, all I do is notice where I am in the Triangle of Connection, and then take one or more escalators as needed. It's *hard* to get friend-zoned this way.

FIRST-DATE IDEAS

....

Pop quiz! Which of these first-date propositions sounds more inviting?

A) "Hey, how about a couple glasses of wine and some stimulating conversation?"

B) "Hey, how about an elaborate, three-hour, white-tablecloth dinner where we sit across from each other, struggle to hold a conversation, and try not to make weird chewing noises?"

Ding, ding! If you picked "A," you're correct! The more fun and low-maintenance you make the date sound, the more likely your potential partner will be into it. Drinks is a classic option, as are coffee, smoothies, or ice cream. Activity dates like bowling, karaoke, or trivia nights can also be a blast and give you built-in stuff to talk about.

For first dates, stay away from doing dinners—they're too expensive and time-consuming, and you're liable to feel stuck if there's no chemistry. No movies or group dates, either. Make it just the two of you.

Avoid big or elaborate gestures. No gifts, poems, or standing outside her window with a boom box playing Peter Gabriel songs. That kind of rom-com stuff reeks of desperation. (There's an *Onion* article titled, "Romantic-Comedy Behavior Gets Real-Life Man Arrested."[2]) I speak from experience. One reason I whiffed with Lisa the first time around was that I tried way too hard. For our second-ever date, I planned a big night out that included tickets to the Empire State Building and a double-decker bus ride. She was visibly annoyed, essentially telling me, "I just wanted to rent a movie and make out, you dolt."

Remember that the most important thing to do on a date is to have fun together. So ideally, you want to choose an activity that you really enjoy doing and that at the same time allows you to connect.

HOW TO ASK HER OUT

....

- Never say, "So, what do *you* want to do?" Women love a man with a plan. Lead!
- Suggest your idea with confidence ("I know a place you're gonna love . . ."), but make sure to listen to any objections she might raise and adjust accordingly.
- Harness the power of the word "let's," which allows you to lead in a non-bossy way ("Hey, let's grab a smoothie . . .").
- Choose a location that's convenient for her to get to.
- Frame it in a way that assumes she'll say yes if she wants to. So, no phrases like ". . . unless you don't want to" or ". . . if you have time."
- Don't start tossing out possible days for the date. If her schedule is busy, she'll have to keep turning you down ("How about Monday? . . . Okay, Wednesday? . . . Maybe Thursday?"), which makes you look too available and too eager. Instead, give her a window of time, and use this magical phrase: "What day(s) works for you?" This way, she'll tell you when *she's* free.
- Add a sweet, sincere comment such as, "It would be cool to finally meet you." Remember: It's not about the wine or the karaoke. It's about the two of you getting closer.

When you put it all together, asking her out will sound something like this: "Hey, Rebecca. You like red wine, so . . . Let's grab a couple glasses this week. I know an awesome spot not far from you. It would be cool to see you. What night works for you?"

BEFORE THE DATE . . .

- On the day of the date, send her a message to make her smile. It can be sincere ("So psyched to meet you tonight") or playful ("I'm at the gym so I'll be totally jacked for our date 💪") or both. This gets you on her mind before the date begins, increasing anticipation.
- Have a second spot in mind where you can go together, if you hit it off.
- If you're going to a bar or coffee shop, arrive fifteen minutes early to make sure you can secure two seats. Grabbing spots at the bar works great. Plan to sit next to her, not across from her. This makes it easier to be physically expressive.
- Text her that you've arrived, and let her know where you are, so she can easily find you. Feel free to add a joke: "I snagged us two stools at the bar. I'm the hottie in the blue shirt fighting off all the single ladies. Better hurry!"
- If she texts you that she's running behind, feel free to tease her: "OK, Miss Tardy—but you owe me a drink for every minute you're late. 😊"
- As you wait for her, don't just surf on your phone. Socialize. Chat up the bartender or the person next to you. This settles your butterflies and gets you in a social mode. When she walks in to see you engaged in conversation, rather than thumb-twiddling and wiping off brow sweat, she'll be impressed.

DURING THE DATE . . .

- Greet her with a friendly hug, not a handshake. It's a date, not a business meeting.
- As a general rule, tease, joke, and flirt early on, and be more "real" and vulnerable as the date unfolds.
- Get in the present moment with her! Follow the three Ps: Be present, positive, and keep things personal.

GAMES PEOPLE PLAY

In dating, you don't want to "play games"—pretending to be hard to get, breadcrumbing, etc. But you do want to play *games*, such as staring contests and Two Truths and a Lie. Games let you romantically connect while having fun. Here are some of my favorite first-date games. (Limit yourself to two per date, or else it seems too gimmicky.)

TWO TRUTHS AND A LIE

You make three statements about yourself, and your date has to guess which is a lie. This game lets you get personal. Choose truths that tee up a funny or revealing story you'd like to share. And ask her to elaborate on her truths.

THE QUESTION GAME

You take turns asking each other *any* question, with one simple rule: You must answer truthfully. Start with innocent questions, and feel free to move toward more adult themes if she's into it.

- *What was your nickname in grade school?*
- *When was the hardest you've ever laughed?*
- *Who was your first kiss?*
- *What's the most trouble you got into in high school?*
- *What's the craziest place you've ever hooked up?*
- *What's your favorite sexual position?*

Notice how the increasingly personal nature of these questions lets you use the first and most important of the Three Romantic Escalators—going from less personal to very personal.

THE FIRST TIME

You ask each other about various "firsts" from your lives—the first time you traveled by yourself, your first kiss, your first concert.

I was once on a date with a sweet, beautiful twenty-two-year-old named Audrey. We'd already shared a nice first kiss when we started to play The First Time. After trading a few questions, I asked, "When was your first kiss?" I was expecting to hear about a grade-school crush. She smiled and blushed. "Oh, about ten minutes ago," she said. *Whoa!* I was her first kiss! I felt . . . honored. I'd been a first-grader and a first husband, but never a first kiss.

When you play fun games, secrets are revealed, and that heightens connection.

Feel free to make up your own games. When my client Doug ("Peter Parker") meets women from Tinder, he and his date might tell people—say, the bartender or people near them on their date—that they met at a bookstore or at a café, sometimes creating a whole backstory. "It's fun because it puts us on the same team," Doug told me.

SEVEN FANTASTIC FIRST-DATE QUESTIONS

There's an old expression: To be interesting, be interested. In a 2017 study, researchers at Harvard found that people who asked questions in one-on-one situations, including first dates, were seen as more likable than those who didn't ask questions.[3] Here are seven questions to ask that will make you downright fascinating and trigger stimulating conversations on dates.

"What's your dream travel destination?" Hey, everyone likes talking travel.

"Who should play you in the movie of your life?" This question caters to your date's ego—and the actress she chooses will clue you in on how she sees herself.

"Who did you see for your first concert?" Music is a great date topic. Prepare to be impressed when she mentions Beyoncé, or saddened when she talks about Nickelback.

"What was the best day of your life?" This question takes your date back in time to a big life moment that she'll love reliving, going much deeper than surface-level chat.

"What do you love most about your job/career?" This one lets you both talk about work in a positive, emotionally evocative way, rather than boringly asking, "What do you do?"

"What were you like as a kid?" Sharing stories from childhood offers her a chance to be vulnerable or tell funny stories.

"What's your hidden talent?" This allows her to show off a bit while also revealing a secret—and sharing small secrets builds trust.

KISS ON YOUR LIST
....

Here's a crash course in how to go for the first kiss.

- **You don't *have* to go for a kiss** on a first date. A date can end with a hug or a kiss on the cheek and get steamier on later dates. Don't force it.
- **If you use the tools in this chapter,** and feel that deep "We" connection, it's weird *not* to go for the kiss. That said . . .
- **You can always use your secret weapon: courage** (one of your Five Super-Values from Chapter 4). It's normal to be nervous before going for the first kiss. Sometimes you just have to be brave and take a chance.
- **If you go for the kiss and she turns a cheek,** don't panic, don't frantically apologize, and don't assume she's not into you. She may not be feeling it *yet* and just needs more time. Or perhaps she's not into PDA.

- **The mere act of going for the kiss can dial up attraction** because it shows you have the guts to take a risk. I've never "lost a girl" by going for a kiss. Yet I lost lots of them by wanting to kiss, but letting fear stop me.

My client Doug had this realization when he brought a date to a live-music venue. "We were playing darts and really vibing, so I leaned in for the kiss, and she pulled away," he said. "But she was smiling. It wasn't a hard 'no.' It was more of a 'not yet.' I held my ground, and I could tell she liked that I went for it, and that I kept my cool. A half hour later, we were sitting in a booth and we just start making out. There's no way that would have happened if I hadn't gone for it earlier."

THREE WAYS TO GO FOR THE KISS

1. **"Close Your Eyes"**
   Look at her, smile, and say, "Close your eyes." If she closes them, that's a green light. Kiss her. If she doesn't close her eyes, no sweat. Try later. You've put the idea of kissing in her mind, which increases sexual tension—and you didn't get the cheek.

2. **The "Shush" Kiss**
   As she's talking, look down at her lips, back at her eyes, and then at her lips again. Smile, softly "shush" her, lean in, and kiss. Post-smooch, say, "I've been wanting to do that all night. You were saying?" Odds are, she won't be able to remember.

3. **Jump Through the "Kiss Window"**
   With enough dates under your belt, your brain will know when to kiss. You'll be able to "read the room." She'll smile a certain way, her eyes will look bigger, she'll be leaning in, and you'll hear that little voice say, *The kiss window's open. Go!* Obey that voice.

HOW TO INVITE HER TO YOUR PLACE

If you want to invite her over, do it. (Reminder: She'll be more likely to say yes if you've escalated logistically and have taken her to at least one other location.) Give her a PG-rated reason to come over—to play Jenga or to meet your dog. It's not about the "thing," of course. It's about spending more time together. But an innocent reason gives her nothing to protest, whereas the phrase "come back to my place" sounds cheesy and has a sexual subtext. Say something genuine like, "I don't want this night to end. Want to come over and [cool thing to do/see/enjoy together]?" If she says yes, great—off you go! If she says no, that's fine, too. It doesn't mean that she's not into you. Many women won't go home with a guy on the first few dates. Be 100 percent cool with it if she declines. She'll appreciate the confidence it took for you to ask. (See Chapter 13 for how to play it when she does come back to your place.)

NINE TEXTS TO SEND THE NEXT DAY (IF YOU WANT TO SEE HER AGAIN)

Funny

- "Last night was great. Do you have a Yelp page where I can leave you a review?"
- "Did you have fun last night? Text 1 for yes, 2 for HELL yes."
- "Mom! Dad! I think I met THE ONE last night. I just hope she doesn't find out that I still live in your basement."

Sweet/Sincere

- "I'm still wearing that smile you gave me."
- "I think we both agree that this needs to happen again, right?"
- "I had this CRAZY dream last night that I met a

cool, awesome, sexy woman who [insert something memorable she said or did]."

Teasing/Cheeky
- "If you promise not to objectify me and treat me like a piece of meat, then I will *consider* going out with you again."
- "Hey, I had a great time last night, but you forgot to pay me. My rate is $1,000 per hour. Is PayPal OK?"
- "Just wanted to let you know that you had a really good time last night and you'd like to see me again."

WHAT TO DO IF YOU
DON'T WANT ANOTHER DATE

If you're not interested in a second date, you don't need to tell her unless prompted. Women are highly intuitive, and she may already sense this. If she messages you, write her back—ghosting is not okay. If she asks you out again, or if she clearly wants you to ask her out, close the door, but do it gently. Tell her it's a chemistry issue, rather than anything about her. Write something like, "I had a great time with you, but the spark wasn't there for me. I know you'll find someone who's as fantastic as you."

WHAT TO DO IF SHE
DOESN'T WANT ANOTHER DATE

As a Radically Authentic man, you're not trying to attract every woman—you're looking for someone who's into your unique vibe. We all have our types. Do *not* misinterpret her lack of interest as evidence that you're unattractive. Summon your Higher Self, wish her well, and move forward. Remember: There are a million more women out there, and you have more to give.

THE SECRET TO FIRST-DATE CONFIDENCE
....

On a first date, confidence comes from focusing on what you can control and influence, and forgetting all else. And you can control a lot, such as . . .

- Picking a great spot, and looking your best
- Leading the conversation in a fun way
- Embracing the Triangle of Connection
- Being Man-to-Woman
- Asking good questions
- Going for the kiss

Focusing on what's outside of your control creates anxiety. But when you dial in on what you can control, you relax, grow confident, and you can influence things like chemistry and connection. For confidence, aim for the bull's-eye of what you can control or influence, and forget everything else.

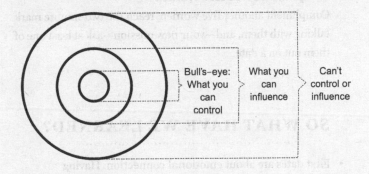

Bull's-eye: What you can control | What you can influence | Can't control or influence

CHAPTER 8 MISSIONS

Three Steps to Great First Dates

1. **Find Your Home-Field Advantage**
    Choose a venue where you'll take some of your dates—a place where you'll feel confident and comfortable and where the staff and regulars know you. (See the Bonus Tip "Use Your Home-Field Advantage.")

2. **Upgrade Your Style**
    Buy a new first-date outfit, focusing on essentials such as pants and shirts that fit great, and on quality shoes. Bring a style-savvy shopper with you to help you choose the outfit, or better yet—ask a woman at the store for her opinion. (See the Bonus Tip "Seven Style Rules for Great First Dates.")

3. **Compliment Five More Women**
    Compliment another five women, reach the two-minute mark talking with them, and—your new mission—ask at least one of them out on a date.

SO WHAT HAVE WE LEARNED?

- First dates are about emotional connection. Having stuff in common is great, but it's more powerful to share emotional commonalities.
- Become an expert at navigating the Triangle of Attraction, which has three levels: "How's the Weather?", "You and Me," and "We." To help you do this, use the Three Romantic Escalators: Verbal/ Personal, Physical, and Logistical.

- You won't "lose the girl" if you go for the kiss too soon, but you may lose her if you wait too long. When in doubt, use courage.
- Remember to have fun! If you light yourself up, you'll light her up.
- Reason no. 322 that you are enough: You're taking action to be a better man, and that propels you to the top tier of men.

⚡ BONUS TIPS ⚡

SEVEN STYLE RULES FOR GREAT FIRST DATES

The right clothes help unlock your confidence. In a *Men's Health* survey, 78 percent of women said that dressing well is the hottest thing a man can do, and 85 percent said that a well-dressed man is sexier than a man with lots of money.[4] Plus, half of feeling attractive is looking attractive.

Here are seven style rules for first dates (and dating in general).

- Your shirts, pants, and jackets should be tailored for your body or appear to be. The biggest style mistake men make? Baggy, ill-fitting clothes. Your duds shouldn't be too tight, nor should they billow. Think somewhat snug.
- Own at least one pair of quality, dark denim jeans (blue or black). And please, no pleated khakis! (Be a hot guy, not a Helpful Honda guy.)
- As for shirts, favor button-downs, polos, and quality tees. In an *Esquire* survey, women preferred plain white tees on a man more than any other kind of shirt.
- Have at least one pair of fun, stylish sneakers (not gym shoes), such as Stan Smiths or Chuck Taylors. As for dress shoes, consider a classic loafer, brogue, or lace-up oxford (brown or black).
- Be well groomed and smell amazing.
- Your hair (or lack thereof) should look "on purpose," whether you're rocking a cool fade or shaving your head. Consider a consultation with a hairstylist. If you're balding, keep it very close-cropped, or go full Kojak.

- Wear boxer briefs. In a *GQ* survey, 65 percent of women preferred boxer briefs on a man (compared to 19 percent for boxers and 5 percent for tighty-whities[5]). True, it's only the first date, but it's best to be prepared.[6]

USE YOUR HOME-FIELD ADVANTAGE

I love the scene in *Goodfellas* when Ray Liotta takes Lorraine Bracco to a nightclub on their first date, and she's wowed by the red-carpet treatment he gets. You can get the same benefit on your dates, without joining the Mafia. Become a regular at a good first-date spot, such as a restaurant, coffee shop, or lounge. Learn the names of the bartenders, the servers, and the manager, and tip well. This will be your "home-field advantage," a place where you feel comfortable, and where a date will see how much others like you. This social approval from people can boost her attraction to you. Once, at my "home-field" bar, I was with a date, and three different people I knew came up to say hi and talk me up. She was borderline starstruck, telling me, "Wow! Everyone loves you!" And I was like, *Fuhgeddaboudit.*

GET YOUR HEAD OUT OF YOUR APPS

HOW TO APPROACH AND CONNECT (PART 1)

**When you have confidence, you can have a lot of fun.
And when you have fun, you can do amazing things.**
—Joe Namath, who never lacked for confidence[1]

Your action failed. Please try again.
—Microsoft Word error message

. . . .

"Sue her? The woman at the magazine rack," I whispered to my client Ray, his forehead a river of sweat. "Go approach her, or it's headlock time."

We were at Barnes & Noble on a Saturday afternoon, and Ray (Higher Self name: "The King"), a shy, smart IT technician, was approaching women. Well, he was supposed to be approaching, but anxiety and doubt were holding him back. He refused to talk to a stylish, blond-haired shopper whose nose was in a copy of *Vogue*. I reminded him of our handshake agreement: "Approach without delay, or I'll do it myself . . . with you in a headlock." Call it tough love.

Duly motivated, Ray took a deep breath, walked over to her and said, "Hi, um, excuse me. I'm Ray, and, um, I just had to say that you're adorable." Her face broke into a huge smile, which relaxed him. They talked for a bit, and he grew more confident. Her name was Emily, and he asked for her number, but she said she was "kinda dating someone." Ray feigned heartbreak: "We only just met and you're already cheating on me?" They laughed and said goodbye on friendly terms.

We took the escalator down one floor for a debrief. "Here's what I loved about that interaction—" I said. But I was interrupted by a tap-tap on Ray's shoulder. It was Emily.

"Hi!" she said to him, her face flush. "I had to come find you. Look, that was the coolest thing that's happened to me in, like, forever. It was so bold. So yeah, you should take my number, if you still want to." They exchanged info and parted ways.

When she was out of sight, Ray erupted: "That! Was! Amazing!"

"No, *you're* amazing," I said. "Do you know why she came looking for you? Most guys just stare at her or catcall. But you walked up to her, all nervous and genuine, like in a Hugh Grant movie. You made her rom-com fantasy come true."

If you're like most single men, you often see women you'd love to meet, yet something stops you from talking to them. What if you could confidently approach that gorgeous woman at Starbucks, or the knockout standing at the bar—and spark interest from the get-go?

To me, approaching is about more than just "getting the girl." It's about freedom. To be able to walk up to a woman and express your most authentic self is liberating. Until you can confidently walk up to a woman and flirt as your real, vulnerable self, there's room to grow.

This chapter will show you how to destroy the fear that keeps you from taking action, so that you can approach with confidence and charm. I'll also give you a simple, universal rule that makes it impossible to fail—one that you can apply today. And in the next chapter, you'll learn a simple framework with all the approach techniques you'll need to help you get phone numbers and dates, day or night, while always being your Higher Self.

APPROACHING IGNITES ATTRACTION

One sunny October afternoon in New York's Flatiron District, I saw a head turner in a red pencil skirt and matching fedora. She was walking on the other side of the street, so I crossed over to meet her. As I was about to say hi, an older guy in a ratty T-shirt shouted, "Damn, girl! God broke the law when he made you!"

I walked alongside her and opened with, "I want to apologize for what my dad just said. He always embarrasses me like that."

She threw her head back and laughed. "You're a *lot* better at hitting on me than he is," she said, stopping to face me. There was immediate mutual attraction.

"I'm Connell."

"I'm Kat."

We talked for ten minutes, about her aspiring singing career and our shared love of improv. We made a date for a few nights later, began seeing each other, and were a couple by Christmas.

Approaching women pays many dividends, such as increasing your dating opportunities and expanding your social comfort zone. But here's something you may not have realized: The very act of approaching can itself ignite attraction. It conveys confidence and vulnerability, two qualities women love in a man.

In fact, I've found that the more beautiful a woman is, the *better* approaching works—when done well. Attractive women get constant attention from men but usually in the form of leers, wolf whistles, and come-ons from creeps. And unfortunately, when good guys do take that chance, they tend to get tongue-tied because they're intimidated by a woman's looks and terrified of rejection. So the rare man who can walk up and be himself—while keeping his nerves in check—becomes magnetic to beautiful women.

Approaching has become a lost art in the Age of Tinder. Women miss it, and they're impressed when a man steps up. If you're the six hundredth guy who's swiped right on a given girl's profile, you won't stand out. But if you walk up to that same woman at the farmers market and charm her, you vault past all the dudes in her dating-app queue.

Some guys ask me: Is it creepy to approach? No! As long as you follow the guidelines in this book.

THE BIG MISTAKE MEN MAKE

There are two seemingly contradictory ways to view approaching:

- It's simple! You casually walk up, chat, and if there's chemistry, you ask her out on a date. If not, it's nothing personal. It's still a win because you took action. OR,
- It's hard! You nervously walk up, struggle for the right words, and if she's not interested, you feel wounded. It's very personal. Because maybe women just aren't into you.

Either of these things can be true. It all depends on your mindset—that is, how you approach approaching.

The majority of men make a costly mistake in this area. They adopt a win-lose paradigm. If she's attracted, success! If she's not, failure. This binary model turns an approach into a high-stakes coin toss: Heads you win, tails you suck. Validation vs. rejection. This amps up the fear factor. You feel like your self-worth is on the line.

I used to see approaching the same way, which is why I never did it. The moment I knew things had to change came when I saw a gorgeous brunette seated by herself at a Starbucks. I wanted to talk to her, but I was in conflict. The angel on one shoulder was rooting me on, but the devil on the other side was talking me out of it.

ANGEL: What a babe! She's your type. Go chat her up.

DEVIL: No! She might think you're creepy.

ANGEL: Creepy? You're a catch. Wouldn't you love to date her?

DEVIL: If she rejects you, it will hurt. A girl like that only dates outgoing guys, not nerdy introverts like you. And all these people will see you get shot down.

ANGEL: Don't listen to him. Walk right over there and tell her AAAAA-HHHGGG—[devil impales angel with pitchfork]

Compare that win-lose mentality to my mindset on the day I met Kat. Sure, I felt some butterflies as I walked up to her, but I had a win-win blueprint that assured success on my own terms: She'll either be attracted to me (win!), or she won't—but I'll feel great for manning up and taking action (win!).

This simple shift in your thinking and focus can change everything. When going out to meet women, you *must* set yourself up to feel pleasure, or else you'll rarely take action. You need reward as an incentive. Now, when a cute girl you've just met bats her lashes and gives you her number, that's a helluva reward, but it's not in your control. There's no guarantee that a given woman will be attracted to you, so you have to set yourself up to "win" no matter how she responds.

At the same time, I urge you to believe in advance that a given approach will go well. It's a Jedi mind trick that's called "assuming attraction." When you walk up to her, assume that a woman will be into you. This positive expectation makes you stand taller and talk louder, often creating a self-fulfilling prophecy. Women can sense that worthiness, that belief, and they like it. When you assume attraction, you get attraction. When you assume rejection, you get rejection.

But as you're about to read, rejection is nothing to fear. It's something to embrace.

THE LIFE-CHANGING MAGIC OF GETTING REJECTED

You don't need to learn how to approach women. You need to learn how to be okay with getting rejected.

Good technique is important but overrated. What you really need is to learn how to get rejected, but *elegantly*. Get rejected and laugh it off. Get rejected and feel good for trying. Get rejected and know that you're still enough. Don't take it personally, or else you might end up with more pain and fear than you started with. The funny thing is, your anxiety will likely peak right before a given approach, and will steadily diminish as you talk (see "Action Model" on the next page). Over time (weeks and months), your fear will decrease as well, until you're left with mere butterflies, not intense anxiety.

There are no quick fixes in this area. Magic bullets only exist in werewolf movies. But destroying your fear of rejection is the closest thing you'll get to an approaching panacea because when that fear disappears, you become free to take action with confidence. And women love confident guys.

The way to destroy that fear of rejection is to let yourself get rejected and learn that it can't really hurt you. Think of it as a vaccine for "fear-of-rejection syndrome." Now, this doesn't mean you purposefully get rejected. It means you stop playing "not to lose" and start playing to win, which means expressing yourself fully and letting the proverbial chips fall.

The very idea of rejection used to horrify me. I thought that being told by a woman to buzz off was proof of my unattractiveness. Whenever I saw a girl I wanted to meet, I fell into the Cycle of Avoidance, which looks like this:

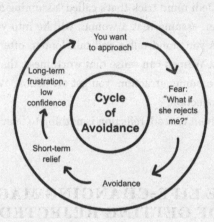

Like me, most single men want to approach but don't. They get stuck in a vicious cycle that provides short-term comfort but long-term pain.

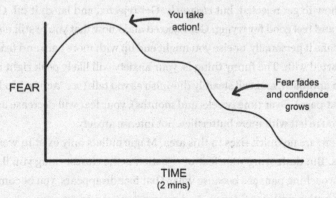

Use courage to break the cycle. It's scary at first, but by the two-minute mark of an approach, you'll feel way more confident!

Instead, you need to use courage (and a few judo moves I'll teach you in the next chapter) to approach, which breaks the cycle and leads both to the results you want and the rejection you *need* to get comfortable accepting.

Your first approaches will likely feel *very* scary to you. Your heart will pound, and your mouth will go dry. But after you do it even a few times, your brain soon realizes that there's nothing to fear. As fear subsides, your confidence rises, and your performance improves.

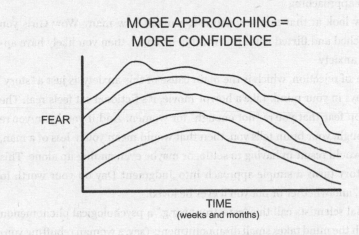

MORE APPROACHING = MORE CONFIDENCE

FEAR

TIME
(weeks and months)

As you approach more and more women, your fear level diminishes. What can feel like suffocating fear at first becomes mere butterflies with time and reps.

WHY APPROACHING FEELS SO SCARY

As mentioned in Chapter 1, there's a very real phenomenon called approach anxiety, which is the feeling of resistance or stress that keeps you from talking to and flirting with attractive women. Approach anxiety is primarily triggered by the pain that you think you will feel if you get rejected: hurt, humiliation, anger, insignificance, and frustration, among other big bads.

Do you have approach anxiety? To find out, let's do some math. I'll bet that in your daily life, certain women catch your eye and make you think,

Wow! Look at her! I call them Wow Girls. In a typical month, how many Wow Girls do you notice on average—at your gym, the bars, on the street, and so on? Next, take that figure, multiply it by twelve, and that's how many Wow Girls you've seen in the last year—likely between three hundred and two thousand, depending on where you live. (If you've recently been in a relationship, simply look at your last twelve months of single life. And you can probably toss 2020 out the window, since COVID-19 put a pretty hard stop on approaching.)

Now look at that number, and ask yourself how many Wow Girls you approached and flirted with. If it was ten or fewer, then you likely have approach anxiety.

Fear of rejection, which is the main cause of this anxiety, is just a "story" that plays in your mind. Like a horror movie, it's fictional yet feels real. The plot: You fear that you're "not enough" for women. And if you learn you're not enough, your brain tells you, then that would mean you're less of a man, which would result in having to settle, or maybe even ending up alone. This scary story turns a simple approach into Judgment Day on your worth to women, and whether or not you'll ever be loved.

Social scientists call this "catastrophizing," a psychological phenomenon in which the mind takes small disappointments (say, a woman rebuffing you) and makes them seem larger than life. Plus, rejection can literally be painful. A 2011 study in the scientific journal *PNAS* concluded that social rejection can "light up" the same parts of the brain that activate when people feel physical pain.[2]

An important note: There's *nothing* wrong with wanting to avoid rejection, or not wanting to "bother" women. These inclinations aren't character flaws. Quite the opposite! They're signs of good mental health, showing that you value your social standing and empathize with women. You just want to eliminate the crippling fear and anxiety that hurts your love life.

BROTHER, CAN YOU PARADIGM?

I want you to redefine rejection. Give it a new meaning. Transform it into something to embrace, or at least not dread.

Your new paradigm? It's a simple, universal rule.

Every approach is a success, because I either get a date, or I put another brick in the cathedral of my character.

Powerful, right? This paradigm turns approaching into a win-win proposition. It sets you up to feel pleasure, rather than pain. It makes it pretty much impossible to "fail," because you've redefined success.

Everything we do is governed by our desire to feel pleasure and avoid pain. If you want to approach women but never do, it's because you don't link enough pleasure to the experience, and you link lots of pain to it.

Imagine an old-timey scale with two plates. One plate represents the pleasure you associate with approaching, and the other plate represents pain. Weighing down the "pleasure" side is connection, confidence, love, sex, finding a girlfriend, etc. But on the "pain" plate, you have rejection, humiliation, feeling creepy, failure, running out of things to say, feeling unattractive, and more. With that much potential pain weighing you down, you either won't approach, or you won't enjoy it if you do.

The fix? Link tons of pleasure to approaching and little, if any, pain. The easy part is brainstorming the feel-good benefits to approaching. What's harder is changing your associations with rejection, which cause the fear of pain. But once you're able to do it and you see that Wow Girl, your brain will quickly run down the upsides and downsides of approaching, and it will look something like this:

UPSIDES TO APPROACHING
- Finding love and connection
- Getting a great girlfriend
- Growing
- More confidence
- More dates
- Great sex
- Making her day better
- Expanding your social skills
- Expressing your true self
- The joy of taking action

- [*cricket noises*]

Okay, maybe there's not *zero* downside. But when you stop linking massive pain to rejection, the "downsides" are negligible—stuff like stumbling over your words or making technical mistakes. (And those problems are fairly easy to fix, as we'll talk about in the next chapter.) This paradigm makes approaching fun because it's all upside and little downside. And that's when you can start to do great things.

A breakthrough for my client Doug, whom I mentioned in the last chapter, came at the grocery store. "I saw this smokin'-hot brunette in yoga leggings," Doug said. "I walked up, looked her straight in the eye, and let her know I was interested. She wasn't into me, but I walked away feeling amazing, just because I had become that guy who can talk to those hotties. Getting blown out like that, it just doesn't bother me anymore. And now I can meet more women and date the ones I have chemistry with."

FOUR NEW WAYS TO
LOOK AT "REJECTION"

1. "Rejection Is a Win." Every approach is a success, even if a girl isn't into you, because you either get a date or you grow as a man. Plus, you're one approach closer to connecting with a wonderful woman.

2. "Rejection Is Part of the Process." It's necessary. Statistically, *most* women you approach won't be into you, but many will be. Hey, Mickey Mantle struck out 1,710 times, but he also hit 536 home runs. You have to swing and miss in order to knock it out of the park.

3. "Rejection Isn't That Bad." I remember the first woman I ever approached: a cute blonde in a cowboy hat. I was so nervous

beforehand. She was clearly not into me but was friendly. I thought, *That wasn't so bad. What have I been so afraid of?*

4. "Rejection Isn't Really Rejection." A woman you just met *can't* truly reject you. She doesn't know you well enough. If your serious girlfriend dumps you for your best friend—okay, *that's* rejection. But if a random woman isn't interested, the worst-case scenario is she's rejecting your technique or your initial "vibe," but not you as a person.

This book is filled with success stories, but to be candid, I've had way more women *not* be into me. That's how I got the wins! Me, I've been turned down more than a Holiday Inn bed, on three continents and in a dozen countries. I don't see these rejections as failures, thanks to the right mindset. Though if I did, it would make for a pretty good blues song.

- *Been blown off in Boston*
- *Shot down in Spain*
- *Jilted in Austin*
- *Called nasty names*
- *I got them rejection blues . . .*

The thing is, I'm not singing the blues (well, anymore) because each so-called rejection thickens my skin, and helps me to learn valuable lessons and to grow. Plus, dating the women who do like me makes those rejections totally worthwhile. Rejection is nothing to fear. It's something to embrace.

Because, as you're about to learn, it's part of the process.

THE RULE OF ONE IN THREE

There's a concept called the Rule of One in Three. When you're Radically Authentic with women, you naturally become polarizing. I don't mean in an intentionally dickish way. You just express yourself in a more raw and real style, which many people will love and some won't. But that's the point.

You don't want to be *kinda* liked by most women. You want to be *loved* by a subset of women.

When you get good at approaching from a truly authentic place, about one out of three girls will be very into you, and two out of three won't be interested at all, at least in a romantic way. At this point, you'll get three kinds of reactions:

- *Hell yes!*
- *Thanks, but no thanks.*
- *Hell no!*

Two-thirds of women won't dig you. Be liberated by this! You can brush off the brush-offs. They're part of the path to finding the women you have chemistry with.

When I first began approaching, I was watering down my personality, being too safe. Lots of women thought I was pleasant and nice, but none wanted to engage much with me, let alone take me home. Once I grew bolder and more authentic, I started to experience the Rule of One in Three— sometimes in a single moment. One night, I boldly walked up to three women who were standing at the bar.

ME: [*with confident vocal tonality*] "You guys are adorable. I had to meet you. Are you friendly?"

GIRL ON LEFT: [*polite but distracted*] "Hey, yeah, we're friendly." *Thanks, but no thanks.*

GIRL ON RIGHT: [*arms folded, frowning*] "I am *not* friendly." *Hell no!*

GIRL IN MIDDLE: [*making penetrating eye contact*] "*You* are cute!" *Hell yes!*

The same dynamic plays out in the daytime, too. One Saturday afternoon, I went out to chat up girls in a park. The first woman was friendly but not interested. The second, a Selena Gomez look-alike, stiff-armed me immediately. Now, most guys would probably quit after two "bad" reactions, but I was following a system, and those interactions were part of the plan. A feature, not a bug.

Next, I went to Whole Foods. In the café section, I saw a tall, thin blonde demonstrating a stand-up yoga pose for a younger girl—her niece or little sister, I assumed. I walked over, mirrored her position, and said, "I didn't know they taught yoga at Whole Foods." They both laughed. Sasha, a Russian-born part-time model and writer, was spending the day with her kid sister. Outright flirting with Sasha would have been weird, so I kept it friendly, talked to both of them, and got Sasha's number.

Understanding the process kept me from taking those first two rejections personally, and led to a date with a tall, blond model-writer—pretty much my dream woman.

Still not convinced? Let's do some math using the Rule of One in Three. If you go out and meet, say, a dozen women in a given week, you can have three or four dates lined up. And the women you meet when approaching tend to be more invested in getting to know you than the girls you meet on the apps, because they've met you in person and experienced your personality firsthand. That means fewer women ghosting you and more women chasing you.

EXCUSES, EXCUSES . . .

I can't stress this enough: Approaching will feel *extremely* scary to you at first, and you will try to talk yourself out of it. You'll see that Jessica Alba look-alike at the bar, walk toward her with the perfect opening line on your tongue, and at the last moment you'll tell yourself, *Gosh, I really need to go do my taxes*, or some such bullshit. That's your Lower Self pouring poison in your ear. Do not listen.

I'm not trying to psych you out. I just want you to be ready when your brain manufactures a "good" excuse not to talk to that Wow Girl. Be ready and chat her up anyway.

EXCUSE: I'm not in the zone.

THE TRUTH: You'll get in the zone after you start talking to her. Approach.

EXCUSE: I'm too busy.

THE TRUTH: It only takes three seconds to say, "Hi, I'm [name.]" Boom! You've just approached. A win, no matter how it goes. Approach.

EXCUSE: I need a drink first.

THE TRUTH: You don't need liquid courage. You need actual courage. Approach.

EXCUSE: She looks busy/isn't in the mood.

THE TRUTH: Everyone's busy. See if you can lift her mood. Approach.

EXCUSE: I don't want to bother her.

THE TRUTH: Her life could be better if you were in it. Approach.

A heads-up: Your Lower Self can find devious ways to keep you in your comfort zone. When I was attending dating seminars, I would sometimes run into a sweet guy named Gerald, whose notebooks were filled with tips. One day, I asked him how his love life was going; with all his notes, I assumed he was meeting lots of women. "I haven't approached anyone yet," he told me. "I'm still learning the theory." Gerald had surely spent thousands of dollars on training but hadn't yet talked to one girl. He was what's called a "seminar junkie."

Beware of that trap. Putting off approaching in order to learn more stuff is a form of creative avoidance. It gives you the illusion of progress without having to be uncomfortable. To get good at approaching, you must approach. Period.

Okay, if you *love* learning dating theory (like me . . . I've written a book on it!), use this rule of thumb: For every hour you spend consuming content, spend an hour "in-field" talking to women/going on dates. You'll improve much faster this way. And practice makes perfect.

Bruce Lee said it best: "If you want to learn to swim, jump into the water. On dry land, no frame of mind is ever going to help you."

BE A 1 PERCENT MAN

When you see an attractive woman you really want to meet, you have three options.

1. **Avoid approaching:** This creates short-term comfort (no rejection) but you'll likely never date the kind of woman you want. I estimate that 95 percent of single men fall into this group.

2. **Approach with a win-lose mindset:** You take action, which is awesome, but the win-lose mentality makes rejection feel painful. And because it feels hard and unpleasant, you only approach once in a blue moon. This is about 4 percent of men.

3. **Approach with a better blueprint:** You use a win-win paradigm. See every interaction as a success, because you either get a date or you grow as a person. This leads to more action and better emotions—and soon, success. This is 1 percent of men.

Are you ready to become a 1 Percent Man?

In the next chapter, I'll teach you the five-step approaching framework to help you lock in the love life you want. Because your next date or girlfriend or great love is out there. She's tired of catcallers and creeps and guys who don't take a chance. She's waiting for an authentic man of action to walk up and give her that rom-com moment.

She's waiting for you.

CHAPTER 9 MISSIONS

Three Steps to Approaching with Confidence

1. **Notice Wow Girls in Your Day-to-Day Life**
   When you see them, ask yourself, *What would I do if I knew I couldn't fail?*

2. **Add Twenty-Five New Great Traits**
   Go back to the "Awesome List" you created in Chapter 3 and write twenty-five *new* traits that make you a great choice for women—and review your original list, too. Keep drawing your confidence from within, rather than needing validation

from others. This list helps you do that. You'll now have fifty reasons why you're enough.

3. **Have a Reject-A-Thon**

Go to a high-traffic area—a bar or lounge at night, or perhaps a shopping center or park in the day—and get rejected five times in a row. The rule? If just one woman responds well, you must go back to zero and start over. (If it helps, bring a wingman and take turns telling the other guy whom he must approach.) Now, don't *try* to make women blow you off by being rude or inconsiderate. Just be normal. You should feel that each rejection stings less and less.

SO WHAT HAVE WE LEARNED?

- Approaching equals attraction. The more beautiful a woman is, the better it works.
- Rejection is not something to fear. It's something to seek out, embrace, and see for what it is: part of the process.
- Beware the win-lose paradigm of approaching that most men use. It sets you up for pain. Decide that every conversation you start with a woman is a success because you either get a date or you build your character. Every approach is a win, an A+ on the report card.
- When you assume attraction, you get attraction. When you assume rejection, you get rejection.
- When you get good at approaching as a Radically Authentic man, about one in three women will be into you, and the rest won't be. Be liberated by this.
- When you approach and get a date, you are enough. When she's not into you, you are still enough—because you took action.

BONUS TIPS

HOW TO RETRAIN YOUR BRAIN

Many scientists believe that our fear of social rejection is a remnant from our evolutionary ancestors. Early humans lived in small groups on the savannahs of East Africa. Back then, being booted from the clan meant likely death, so we evolved to fear social rejection.

The human brain is about a million years old. (Though it doesn't look a day over half a mil.) But now, instead of *Don't get eaten by a saber-tooth tiger*, your mind tells you, *Don't get rejected by a girl*. So when you walk up to that woman at the bar, your fight-or-flight response kicks in. Cue the sweat, racing heart, and dry mouth.

The solution? Approach and show your brain that there's no real risk. Some of my clients' hands are shaking before they talk to that first woman of the night. An hour later, they're laughing, flirting, and setting up dates.

WHEN SHOULD YOU FEEL REJECTED?

When you consistently fail to take action. That's the only real rejection to fear, because it means you rejected yourself. Link pleasure to getting "rejected" by women and pain to rejecting yourself.

THREE WAYS TO STAY
CONFIDENT WHEN APPROACHING

The words we use impact our emotions. The next time some-one asks you how you're doing, instead of mumbling, "Could be worse," say, "I'm absolutely *amazing*." In fact, say that phrase out loud right now—even if people are around you. Go!

Did you notice how saying those words juiced your self-confidence a bit? Certain words carry strong meanings, so when you use empowering words, you feel more confident.

Here are three ways to harness the power of language—and boost your confidence—when out meeting women.

Pepper your conversations with words that make you feel good, such as: "awesome," "amazing," "spectacular," "incred-ible." This will make you feel more charismatic and positive.

After every approach, ask yourself one question: What was awesome about that approach? And use that word: "awesome." This links good vibes to every conversation you have.

Avoid using the word "rejection" when you're out meeting women. I've only used the R-word here for teaching purposes. I avoid it when I'm wingmanning my clients because the word is weighted with negativity. Instead of "rejection," call an approach that goes nowhere a "blowout." As in, "I went up to that girl, but she totally blew me out." Or, "She was loving me, but her friend took her away. Blowout!" A rejection stings. A blowout is funny because it's hyperbolic, conjuring images of bursting car tires or flaming oil wells. It's exaggeration to the point of absurdity, which keeps you feeling loose. When you're out "in the field," there is no rejection. Only blowouts. And blowouts are *awesome*.

TOOLS & TECHNIQUES

HOW TO APPROACH AND CONNECT (PART 2)

Call me maybe.
—Carly Rae Jepsen

....

I walked toward her, the girl in the sleek silver dress, knowing exactly what to say.

Before this night, I had been in a rut. I'd been going out to meet women for several months, but I wasn't doing much approaching. I'd see someone, try to think of the perfect thing to say, and do nothing. Either that or I would make a half-assed effort—a meek "hello"—that led to a quick rejection. At one club, I spent half of the night hiding in the men's room so I wouldn't have to try at all.

This Saturday night would be different. I had a framework. A system. My only goal? Follow two rules: Talk to lots of women, and always say what I feel. I needed more action and less filter.

When the elevator doors opened to the rooftop lounge, I walked up to the first person I saw. No checking my phone, no trips to the bar. See girl, talk to girl, speak my mind. Wash, rinse, repeat.

An hour in, I saw the woman in silver—a brunette with curly hair. I made a beeline toward her.

Say what you feel, I told myself. *Be real.*

"Hi," I said. "I'm actually pretty shy, but I just had to meet you." Not clever but sincere. The words came out with a crispness that surprised me.

"Yeah, sure, you're *real* shy," she said with a smile, her greenish-gray eyes popping. "Hi! I'm Brie."

This was new. I had never led with this kind of vulnerability, and I had never gotten such a positive initial reaction. By being real, inside and out, I felt aligned—like a revving car engine in perfect balance. Brie saw a charismatic guy with a smooth line, not an introverted dweeb with approach anxiety. Hey, as long as she liked it.

Keep going, I told myself. *Speak your thoughts.*

"You have awesome eighties hair," I said. "Were you in the Bangles?"

She laughed. "I love the Bangles!"

"Who doesn't love the Bangles?"

"I play eighties music at my classes. I'm a dance teacher."

Tell the truth. Express, don't impress.

"You need to teach me," I said. "I suck at dancing. I can do the robot. That's about it. I'm so white."

"Dancing is all *here*," she said, rolling her hips and ending with a hair flip.

"Now you're just trying to turn me on."

"Is it working?" She laughed.

"This place is so unsexy next to you." Not a bad line. It came out of the moment.

Lead, lead, lead. Women like guys who lead.

I took her hand and brought her to the dance floor. Two songs in, we were kissing. It had been only ten minutes since I approached.

She had to meet up with friends, so I got her number, and we set up a date for another night.

Walking home later, I felt buzzed, even though I hadn't had a drop of booze. *This is how it's done,* I thought. *Fully commit to the approach and to the process. It's all about the process.*

I checked my phone. A message from Brie: "Great meeting u! Can't wait till Thurs ;)"

You now have the mindset it takes to approach and connect with wonderful women as the real you. In this chapter, I'll give you the needed techniques, whether you want to meet girls when you're out at night or when you're going about your day. You'll also learn a framework called the Five Master Steps that makes approaching fun and effective, so that you always know what to say and how to say it.

THE FIVE MASTER STEPS

When you go out to approach, you need a framework that gives you certainty and structure. Your brain craves certainty, but dating is filled with things outside of your control. You can't count on any given woman liking you, but you can count on a system that leads to lots of women liking you over time. Just as top athletes like LeBron James follow a routine to assure success, you need to follow an approaching routine that leads you to romantic connections.

I teach a framework that I call the Five Master Steps.* When you go out, day or night, your primary goal is *not* to get "results." Your primary goal is to follow the Five Master Steps. This helps you focus on the process and keeps you from being creepily results-focused. (A woman doesn't want to be a guy's "result." She wants to be with a guy who's genuinely enjoying her.)

Important! When you go out to apply this system, commit to a minimum amount of time—at least thirty minutes, but ideally an hour or more. Treat it like going to the gym. The more time and effort you put in, the better. But don't overdo it, either. Make a one-hour session following the Five Master Steps your sweet spot.

YOUR STEPS TO SUCCESS

1. **Open Often**
   Talk to lots of women, not waiting too long between interactions.

---

* A shout-out to Owen Cook, a former mentor of mine who taught me more about approaching than anyone else. My framework is based in part on what I learned from him.

2. **Offer Authentic Value**
   Be you. You are enough.

3. **Make a Connection**
   It's about connection, not attraction.

4. **Go for It!**
   A number, a date, a kiss. Go for what you want.

5. **Appreciate Something Great**
   Notice at least one awesome thing about every approach.

Let's dig in deeper.

I: OPEN OFTEN

When you're out to meet women, make sure you actually meet women! Start *lots* of conversations. Talk to someone new at least every five to ten minutes at night and every fifteen minutes during the day. This may sound like a high bar if you're introverted, like I am. But once you dive in and start, it's actually *easier* to talk to, say, a dozen women in a night than to only approach one or two and be shoved in your head the rest of the time. Taking action gets you out of your head and gives you social momentum, unlocking your Higher Self. You become present.

In a perfect world, you won't approach the entire time. You'll hit it off with a woman you like and hang with her. But if this doesn't happen at first, don't sweat it. Stick to the steps and go home feeling incredible for being a man of action who's getting better with women every day.

When you follow this first step and open conversations with a lot of girls—I'm talking five to ten in one hour in a busy bar at night—you'll notice a shift in your psychology. What happens is, the fearful part of your brain switches off, and you see true opportunity rather than false danger. This leads to bolder actions and some badass benefits. You enter a fearless flow state that feels like being slightly drunk, yet you're completely clear-headed. It's your Higher Self fully activated, and it's addictive. (To learn how and why our brains enter this state, read *Flow: The Psychology of Optimal Experience*, by Mihaly Csikszentmihalyi.)

When you "open often" and get into a nice flow state, cool things happen. I dated a woman in L.A. whom I'd met when I approached her at a cocktail party at a W Hotel. After our first night together, we were lying in bed and she said, "I was so impressed the way you came right up to me, even though I was with Mike," referring to a burly guy friend she had been talking to when I first said hello. The truth is, I barely even noticed Mike—at least, not as a threat. I could only see the upside.

Again, your Lower Self will try to talk you out of that first approach. Simply decide to take action. You're more likely to act your way into right thinking than to think your way into right acting.

2: OFFER AUTHENTIC VALUE

Simply put, be you, and try to make her day/night better than before she met you. Here are three ways to do that.

- Be Man-to-Woman. Flirt. Let her know you're interested. That said . . .
- Be sincere. Not everything has to be a "move." Quite the opposite. M-W is the pepper in the dish. The main course is your authentic personality. Because (all together now) you are enough.
- Be fun. Crack jokes. Show your playful side. Dating should be fun, and so should approaching. This will help you a lot, both in terms of enjoying the process and hitting it off with the kinds of women you're attracted to.

If you go out, flirt a bit, be sincere, and have fun on your own terms— that's really all you have to do! It can be that simple.

Most guys are not their true selves with women, and they're trying to take rather than give. Owen Cook, my approaching coach from back in the day, used to say, "A hot girl at a club is like a millionaire, and most men are paupers with their hands out." Not you. You're that rare guy who approaches her with the intention to give, not to take. You're at her level. The guy who offers authentic value.

And when you give to women, women love to give back.

3: MAKE A CONNECTION

Look for things you have in common and share emotional experiences, as I mentioned in Chapter 8. A former dating coach of mine gave me a great tip that I still use: "Find out what makes her fascinating." If a woman feels that you "get" her, she'll feel more connected to you.

Lots of guys want her. You'll be the guy who understands her, and that's way more powerful.

4: GO FOR IT!

If you like her, go for what you want—a number, a date, a dance-floor make-out. Don't settle for just a nice conversation. Lead things somewhere. It's about playing to win, rather than playing not to lose.

One summer afternoon, I was wingmanning for my client Michael (Higher Self name: "Magic Mike"), thirty, who was on a park bench talking to a woman he'd just met. I left for a few minutes, and when I got back, she was alone. I found Michael sitting not far away, his shoulders slumped, his face in his hands.

"What happened?" I asked.

"I screwed up," he said. "It was going great, but I chickened out and didn't ask her out. I just left. I suck!"

"It's all good," I said. "She's still there. It's not too late. Let me ask you—if you went back over there, what would you say to her if you knew you couldn't fail?"

"I would tell her that I wimped out because I got scared, but that I'd love to take her out."

"Perfect," I said. "There she is. Go!"

He reapproached her. I couldn't hear the conversation, but I saw her look up, listen, smile, and extend her hand, asking for his phone. Numbers exchanged, date set.

Your Lower Self will try to talk you out of taking risks. Don't let it. Don't settle for just a nice conversation. Go for it!

5: APPRECIATE SOMETHING GREAT

After *every* approach—whether it lasted three seconds or three hours—appreciate at least one great thing about it. A joke you made, a lesson you learned. Or, if you got blown out, see something funny in it.

Approaching success is largely about managing your emotions, and Step 5 keeps you focused on the positive and empowering rather than on judging yourself. What you focus on is what you will feel, so focus on something empowering.

Do. Not. Skip. This. Step. If you do, you'll turn into Judge Judy, finding every flaw, real or imagined, in your interactions. I know. I did that for years. (See: "Elevator Wall, Connell Slamming Head Against," Chapter 4.) Remember: Every approach is a win. No self-judgment allowed.

These are the Five Master Steps. This tested system assures that you'll meet lots of women as the real you. If you apply it, it's hard *not* to hit it off with some wonderful women.

THE FOUR AND A HALF MASTER STEPS

Most guys love these steps, but some aren't crazy about approaching girl after girl. I get it. It takes a lot of effort. So here's a tweaked version for you to test-drive. Call it the Four and a Half Master Steps.

It works like this. Steps 2 to 5 are identical, but Step 1 is different. Instead of going out for an hour or more and opening tons of conversations, you only talk to women who inspire something in you. That is, you see a Wow Girl and you say, *I'm going in!* even if you haven't approached a woman in a week. You go about your life feeling no pressure to approach. But when you do see that head-turning woman, you decide to talk to her . . . and finish the rest of the steps.

Two caveats: This modified system doesn't give you the momentum that comes with opening often, and it doesn't give you many reps. More girls approached equals more girls dated. So be prepared: You'll likely feel more fear when you see that Wow Girl. The fix? Good old-fashioned courage, nerves be damned.

THE TOOLS OF THE TRADE

When you approach a woman, there are a few basic mechanics you want to have handled.

Good Vocal Tonality: The way you use your voice signals your confidence level to a woman. Whether you're in a cacophonous club or a quiet coffee shop, make sure your voice meets or slightly exceeds the baseline conversational noise level of the environment. A soft, passive tone will likely bring on a swift rejection. But a resonant, confident voice tells a woman that you're a man of value, making her think, *Wow, who's this confident guy?*

Eye Contact: Make it laser-like. This conveys authority, trust, and warmth.

Smile: A small, sly grin is best. Smiling ear to ear can make you seem too eager, and a scowl is too intense.

Good Posture/Body Language: Stand nice and tall. Also, take up "space" with your body, especially in a bar. Widen your stance and throw your shoulders back. You'll look and feel more confident because your physiology affects your emotions.

THE ART OF OPENING

When you open a conversation, it's not as much what you say as *how* you say it. You need full commitment. An opener that tanks on Tinder ("Hi, how are you?") can work great in person (that is, if you *fully* commit), because IRL she experiences all of your behavioral cues.

Your opener does *not* have to be clever or fancy—just good enough to get her to respond. I've begun conversations with openers as simple as these:

- Hi.
- You have great style.
- How's your night going?
- I feel awesome today, and I had to share it with you.
- What book are you reading?
- Is this the coolest club around here?
- Whoa, this line is long.

Being clever or funny is a nice bonus, but it's just not necessary. Simple and clear is best. My client Oscar was having a drink with friends at a

Miami lounge when he saw Anastasia, a tall, intelligent pharmaceutical rep. He approached her, they liked each other, and later left the bar together. The next day, his impressed (and envious) buddy asked Oscar what he said to Anastasia. What amazing opener did he use on her? Oscar explained, "I just said, 'Damn, who are you?' My vibe was, 'I'm into you. You into me? Cool. Let's get outta here.' I'm a man, and she's a woman. Why would it *not* be like that?"

Oscar used what's called a direct opener. Every opener falls into one of two categories: direct and indirect.

DIRECT OPENERS
....

"Going direct" means that your words and/or vibe convey clear romantic interest from the get-go. Here are examples of direct openers.

- Hi, I saw you and had to meet you.
- You're absolutely adorable.
- Wow. You're gorgeous. Who are you?
- I'm here to flirt with you.
- You're sexy.

Upside: There's no chance of the friend zone. Whether or not she's attracted to you, she'll know why you're talking to her. Lots of women love direct men, so it can ignite instant interest, like when I approached Brie. And it can feel freeing to shed weighty expectations and just be real with women from the start.

Downside: It's a polarizing technique, so plenty of women will reject you right away. If she's not available or just not in the mood, she'll hold up a big, fat stop sign. Either sparks will fly or *she* will—as she walks away.

Quick Tip: Directness is not a license to be vulgar. If you go direct, don't make it about her body, and don't say anything about sexual acts. "You're sexy" is about as blunt as you want to be.

INDIRECT OPENERS

....

"Going indirect" means that you don't explicitly state romantic interest up front. You might make small talk or give her a compliment that's more friendly than flirty. You don't hide your intentions; you just don't lead with them. Here are some indirect openers.

- How's your night going?
- I dig your boots/jacket/style.
- Isn't this song great?
- How's that book you're reading?
- Your hair looks amazing.

Upside: It opens the door to a *lot* more conversations since you don't get as many blowouts. This helps you gain experience, build confidence, and talk to more women, which gives you more dating opportunities. In terms of starting interactions, going indirect gives you a much higher batting average.

Downside: Because the context is initially more Friend-to-Friend, some men get stuck in the "friendly guy" mode, which hurts their chances of creating a romantic spark. If you open in this way, you still need to flirt and be M-W fairly soon.

Quick Tip: After you open, within a minute or two, start to pepper the conversation with a flirty comment or two, such as . . .

- "Wow, you have a sexy laugh. Anyway . . ."
- "What do you do, when you're not making handsome men flirt with you?"
- "No way, you're into [hobby]? You're not just pretty. You're actually cool."

Which Opening Style Should You Use?
Try both, see what feels most like you, and go with what women enjoy the most.

SO, SHE'S TALKING TO YOU . . . NOW WHAT?

It's simple: Keep the conversation about you and her. (See Chapter 8, on great first dates.)

Now, if you used an indirect opener, you can talk for a bit about the icebreaker topic—say, the book she's reading or boots she's wearing. Then change subjects. A simple way to do that is to introduce yourself and shake hands (assuming hand-shaking returns in our post-COVID world). This lets you bridge to the next topic.

After a direct opener—such as "I had to meet you"—you have a couple of options. You can literally say whatever enters your mind, like when I complimented Brie's hair. Or, you can introduce yourself.

It's fine to ask questions, but try to make them open-ended, rather than yes-or-no. And don't forget Step 2: Offer Authentic Value. Talk about you. Make statements. Some guys interrogate women while sharing nothing about themselves. That won't work.

AND NOW FOR THE PLAY-BY-PLAY!

Here's a conversation I had with Nicole, a woman I approached on a cold January day in a grocery store. (My director's commentary is in bold.)

ME: Excuse me, miss. You look like the cover of J.Crew's winter catalog. Super cute. **She was bundled up in a pink scarf and fuzzy white hat. This is a direct opener.**

NICOLE: [*smiling*] Oh, hi, thanks. I got the scarf for Christmas.

ME: Nice. How was your holiday? Get anything good? **That may sound like a boring question, but after a direct opener, you don't need to do much. Normal, relatable chitchat is better than forcing funny lines.**

NICOLE: My mom gave me a spa treatment and a bunch of gift certificates.

ME: My dad *hates* gift cards. He's such a Scrooge. But I'm the youngest of six, so I always get what I want. **I've offered info about me after asking about her. You want a balance.** I'm Connell, by the way. It's a pleasure.

NICOLE: I'm Nicole! Nice to meet you. **Always introduce yourself.**

ME: So what do you do? Wait, let me guess. I'm gonna say you work in fashion. **It's fun to try to guess what a woman's job is. Games are fun!**

NICOLE: Not even close. I do social media for [company name], but we sometimes work with fashion brands. What do you do?

ME: I'm a magazine journalist. I write about golf. **I make a golf-swing motion. Using hand gestures can make you appear more charismatic.**

NICOLE: My dad loves golf! I'm not that into it, but I love to drive the cart.

ME: Just my luck. Pretty girls like you never play golf. It's always the dads. **"Pretty girls like you" is another M-W statement. I've done more than enough to keep things flirty. We talk about salad for the next two minutes. Then, it's time to go for a date! I still get nervous at this part, but I just go for it.**

ME: I have to go in a second, but I'm really glad we met. You're really cool—even though you hate golf. **Just a little tease.**

NICOLE: It was nice meeting you, too.

ME: It would be nice to meet up when we're not shopping.

NICOLE: Yes, I'd like that.

ME: How about a drink this week? What night is good for you? **Try to arrange the date during the interaction. Getting it on her calendar right away cuts down on ghosting and flaking because people like to be consistent with their commitments.**

NICOLE: I can do Wednesday or Thursday night?

ME: I'm free Thursday. Let's do eight. Are you more into cocktail lounges or dive bars?

NICOLE: Hmm. I like both, but I'm down with cocktails.

ME: Okay, I'll find a good spot and I'll text you. What's your number? **I take her number and stay for another minute. Why do I stay? If you bolt right away, she might feel that it was just about getting her number, like it's a trophy. Hang in for another minute and talk about *anything*: the weather, spelunking, the Spanish Civil War. Don't be a phone-number bandit!** Hey, it was great meeting you. I can't wait till Thursday.

NICOLE: Thanks! You, too. I mean, *me* too! [*laughs*]. **She's nervous and flustered. So dang cute.**

ME: You're adorable. Bye.

When you get a woman's number, send her a sweet text message the same day. (No need to wait or "play it cool.") This solidifies the date, if you made one, and puts a smile on her face. That night I texted her: "Nice meeting you, J.Crew model, aka Nicole . . . I'll text you deets for Thurs. ;) —Connell"

Okay, let's review this interaction through the lens of the Five Master Steps. Before I met her that day, I had been **opening often**, which put me in a social, outgoing mood. By opening directly and being me, I **offered authentic value**, which helped me **make a connection** right away. I decided to **go for it** and ask for a date. And in terms of **appreciating something great**, I was happy with my opener—and of course, landing a date.

HOW TO GET AN INSTANT-DATE

When you approach and hit it off, day or night, you have two main options: Get her number and meet another time, or take her on an instant-date right away.

During the day, going on an instant-date is very possible because women tend to be by themselves. You could go from an approach to a coffee/smoothie/drink in minutes. All you do, as a lead-up to Step 4, is ask her, "What are you doing right now?" If you're both free, suggest a date right then. There's no time like the present. If she's busy, then take her number, ideally setting up a date for later.

But in the evening, leaving a bar or club with a woman is a more complex process. If you want to walk into a venue at night and walk out with a woman on your arm, you need to get good at "handling logistics."

IT'S ALL ABOUT LOGISTICS

Learning a woman's logistics—details such as who she's with, where she lives, and what she's doing later—is essential if you want an instant-date at night. A woman can be into you, but if she has "bad" logistics (say, she's the designated driver of a bachelorette party), there's no way she's leaving the venue with you.

Good logistics: She's out by herself (very rare), has nothing planned for later, can sleep in tomorrow, and lives nearby. Go for the instant-date.

Bad logistics: She's part of a large group, has dinner plans later, or is on a 9 a.m. flight in the morning. Take her number and schedule a date for a different time.

Her logistics will likely fall between those two extremes. Here are three questions to ask her during your interaction to help you know the score.

1. **"Who Are You Here With?"**

   A woman you meet at night is almost always with people. You need to know if she's with her serious boyfriend, her female friend, her rabbi, etc.

   Related note: If you like her, make sure you meet and befriend her friends. If her crew approves of you, that helps you with her.

2. **"How Do You Know Each Other?"**

   This clarifies the dynamics of her peer group, giving you valuable intel. Are they sisters? Friends? Coworkers? Always ask *her* this question. Never ask a guy in the group. Men will lie ("She's dating me") to try to get rid of you, even if they're not a couple.

   Don't assume a guy is her boyfriend. As I mentioned in Chapter 3, my client Robert and I were at a lounge when we met Sofia. The handsome guy she was with? Her brother. Armed with this knowledge, I occupied the brother while Robert and Sofia got *very* close. At one point, Sofia placed Robert's hands on her chest and said, "Of course they're real. Feel them!" I kept her brother distracted, with his back turned to his sister. (Weirdest. Job. Ever.)

3. **"What Are You Doing Later/Tomorrow?"**

   Before you suggest an instant-date, make sure she's available—that is, she has no late-dinner plans, or isn't waking at dawn for yoga class.

HOW TO SUGGEST AN INSTANT-DATE

If her logistics are good, there are three keys to getting an instant-date:

- Suggest something fun, with confidence. ("Hey, you know what would be awesome? I know this cool little jazz bar . . .")
- Make it easy to get to. (". . . and it's a five-minute cab ride.")
- Prepare to hear this objection. "I can't leave my friends." That's totally normal. Feel free to ask again later, when she may be ready for a change of scene, or after her friends have peeled off.

PEER PRESSURE

So, you're out at night and vibing well with a cool woman. Who knows where things will lead? Just watch out for the three people who can block your . . . um . . . success.

THE FEMALE FRIEND

Who They Are: A person in her crew.
How to Handle Them: Introduce yourself. Be sincere and friendly, yet unapologetic about your interest in her. Typically, her girlfriends *want* her to meet someone like you. If you get the friend(s) on your side, the woman you like will be impressed.

THE COCKBLOCK

Who They Are: A jealous male friend.

How to Handle Them: Beware of the jealous male friend who feels, *If I can't date her, no one can.* Create rapport with and compliment him, without supplicating, of course. Better yet, introduce him to a different cute girl! He'll appreciate the wingman work.

(Side note: In the interest of gender equality, we need a female-forward term to join "cockblock" in the no-sex lexicon. After discussing this with my photographer Riane, we suggest "va-jay-nay," "cliterference," and "taco blocko.")

THE APPROACH CRASHER

Who They Are: A guy who interrupts your interaction to try to steal your girl.
How to Handle Them: First, don't panic. She likes you, not him. If he has weak "game," be civil for a minute or two, then say, "It was nice meeting you—we're gonna get back to our conversation." Then focus on her and ignore him. Deprived of social oxygen, he'll likely leave.

But if he's funny and outgoing, watch out. He *could* steal her from you. Get you and her outta there. Decisively tell her, "Let's go check out [other part of venue]," take her hand, and go. This puts Mr. Smooth in a no-win situation: He'll either follow you like a stalker, which will creep her out, or he'll stay put, in which case you've lost him. Check and mate.

THE PARADOX OF APPROACHING: SAFE IS RISKY AND RISKY IS SAFE

When you approach, you *must* fully commit. She needs to hear you and see you. I don't care if she likes you or not—just make sure she reacts to you.

You're doing it right if it feels risky. Follow that feeling! The paradox is, an approach that feels "risky" is actually safe, because full commitment is how you get results. Think Jack Nicholson committing to a role, or Michael Jordan committing to driving to the hoop. On the flipside, a "safe" approach is very risky because it won't work.

When I approached Brie, I fully committed. I walked up, looked her in the eye, and said something vulnerable. I didn't half-ass it. I used my entire ass (what little there is of it).

Safe: Seeing a Wow Girl, trying to think of the "perfect" opener, and watching her walk away.

Risky: Saying something—anything!—that enters your mind, even just "Hi."

Safe: Opening with a soft, whispery vocal tonality that creeps her out.

Risky: Using a clear, LOUD, resonant tone that makes her notice you.

Safe: Having a great conversation, but not asking for her number.

Risky: Going for it! The only way to get dates is to ask for dates.

Remember: Safe is risky, and risky is safe.

Be risky.

SEVEN COMMON APPROACH PROBLEMS . . . SOLVED!

1. **How Can I Tell if She's Interested?**
    The telltale sign: She's attentive and makes good eye contact. Giggling and hair-twirling are great, but if she's attentive, that's the best sign. And don't worry if she's a little quiet at first. She might just need time to warm up to you.

2. **What's the Most Common Mistake Guys Make When They Approach?**
    Not talking loudly enough, which can get you rejected instantly. Yet it's an easy fix, once you're aware of it. Here's two tips to help.
    - Gesture with your hands and arms while you speak. Boldness with your body can dial up the decibels of your voice.
    - Right before you go out to approach, put a favorite song on your phone and belt it out loud, karaoke-style. Make sure others can hear you. This helps you loosen up, leading to better tonality.

3. How Do I Approach the 9s and 10s?

Any number you label a woman with is in *your* head, not hers. The so-called 9s and 10s don't strut through life thinking about their numeric worth.

That said, model-caliber women do hear "You're hot" (and the like) all the time. Set yourself apart with a fun, playful opener—something that makes *you* laugh. At a nightclub one night, I saw a woman I wanted to meet, and I knew I needed to be different from all the guys who were fawning over her. I unbuttoned my shirt halfway to expose my chest, walked up to her, and said with an exaggerated Latin Lover accent, "*Buenas noches*. I am . . . *Armando*." She cracked up, and we eventually left the club for an instant-date. (She called me Armando for weeks.)

4. How Do I Ask for Phone Numbers?

Don't ask. Assume. After you've been talking for a few minutes, say, "Let's exchange numbers" or "What's your number?" Then take out your phone, certain she'll follow your lead.

Also, at night, it's easy to be into a woman, get separated, and never see her again. So, ask for a number sooner rather than later. Go for her number in under ten minutes. This way, if you lose sight of her, you can stay in touch and meet up another time.

5. Can I Approach Her if She's Busy?

Depends on how busy she is, on a scale of "typing on laptop" to "landing a 747." Use common sense. If she's wearing headphones, no biggie. Gesture for her to take them out. (You're potentially much more important to her life than that podcast.) But if she's on the phone, don't interrupt her. It's rude.

When you do approach a woman who's occupied, acknowledge that you get that she's busy. It shows empathy, and women notice that. My buddy Ted and I were at a Brooklyn restaurant waiting for a table, and he saw how taken I was with a waitress who was swamped. I didn't want to bother her (that sneaky Lower Self!), but Ted gave me a great opener. As she walked by, carrying a tray of brunch specials, I said, "How cool would a guy have to be to make you stop working for one minute and talk to him?"

"He'd have to be pretty cool," she said with a laugh. It didn't go anywhere, but I saw a flicker of respect in her eyes, if not attraction, and it felt great to try. Every approach is a win!

6. **Where Should I Approach in the Daytime?**
Seek a high-traffic area, such as a park or mall. This makes it easier to bounce from one interaction to another.

7. **When I Meet a Woman at Night, What's the Best Way to Get Her Back to My Place?**
I have a crazy take on this: Ask her!

Be transparent. Never hide your intentions or try to manipulate her. It's dishonest and ineffective. Once, while leaving a club with a girl I had just met, I took a pickup coach's advice and gave her intentionally vague details about where we were going. "I'm taking you someplace you will love," I said as we got in a cab, implying that we were heading to another bar. When we pulled up in front of my apartment building, she was disappointed. "You know, you could have just invited me over," she said. "I would have said yes." I felt sketchy.

When you want to invite a woman you just met to come back to your place, do two things. First, invite her to another spot—grab another drink, go get pizza—so that you can both get more comfortable with each other. And as things are winding down there, be sincere. Say, "I'm having so much fun with you, and I don't want the night to end. Want to come over and [fun, PG-rated thing you can do]?" It's not about the "thing," of course. It's about the two of you getting more time together.

CHAPTER 10 MISSIONS

Three Steps to Getting Numbers and Dates

1. **Follow the Five Master Steps**

   Find a high-traffic area (like a park, mall, or bar) and use the Five Master Steps to open conversations with women (at least four) over the course of sixty minutes. Once you complete this mission . . .

2. **Celebrate!**

   You can now talk to women as your real, authentic self. You're now in the top 1 percent of men. This is big. It's worth celebrating.

3. **Find Wingmen**

   Look for like-minded single guys to become your wingmen when you go out, and who can hold you accountable as you work on your dating goals. And join my Facebook group to instantly connect with me and thousands of single men.

SO WHAT HAVE WE LEARNED?

- When you go out to approach, day or night, you need a framework that gives you certainty and structure. The Five Master Steps provide that framework.
- You can start conversations in two ways: with direct or indirect openers.
- Full commitment when you approach is a must. Playing it safe is actually risky, while being risky is safe.
- Don't force being witty or clever when talking to a woman—know that whatever you say is enough because *you* are enough.

⊱ BONUS TIPS ⊰

HOW TO OPEN CONVERSATIONS
WITH WOMEN . . . ANYWHERE

Pay her a sincere, specific compliment, based on something you notice and like. Make sure it's authentic and specific. (During the day, you might preface your opener with a gentlemanly "Excuse me, miss . . ." That sort of nicety isn't needed at night.) Some examples:

> I really like your tattoo. It's edgy.
>
> You have great style. Love the leather boots.
>
> You have a very confident walk.

THREE WAYS TO NEVER
RUN OUT OF THINGS TO SAY

Lower the bar for how good your conversation has to be. Guys struggle because they think they have to be witty and clever. (Have you ever "run out of things to say" with your sister, cousin, or female friends?) Express, don't impress. Anything you say is enough because *you* are enough.

During a conversation, ask her open-ended questions, which tend to start with the words what, why, how, or where. Here's an example of each:

What do you love most about [her hobby/interest/job]?

Why did you move to/visit [city]?

How did you and your friend meet?

Where would you live if you could go anywhere?

If all else fails, take a deep breath and ask yourself, *What am I thinking/feeling?* and say that! Yes, even if it ends up being, "I'm not sure what to say—pretty girls make me nervous." She will *love* that level of vulnerability.

HOW TO START YOUR NIGHT RIGHT

The hardest approach of the night will *always* be the first one. To properly kick off the Five Master Steps, do the following. As soon as you walk into a venue, talk to literally the first person you see—woman, man, couple, alien life-form. Anyone! This will help you shift into "social" mode, making it much easier to chat up the next person.

CHAPTER 11

ADVANCED NINJA MOVES

Bandit: I just go from place to place and do what I do best.
Carrie: What's that?
Bandit: Show off.
—*Smokey and the Bandit*[1]

....

I saw her in the grocery store. She was holding a yoga mat, and I noticed a pack of Camels peeking from her jean-jacket pocket. I walked up and said, "Wow, you're a woman of contradictions. The yoga gear says 'fitness nut,' but the smokes say 'emphysema.'"

She laughed. "Yeah, I guess I'm sending mixed signals. I'm trying to quit."

"You're just complex, like a sexy Walt Whitman—you contain multitudes." She laughed. "Hi, I'm Katie," she said, introducing herself first, a sign of interest. But I sensed some awkwardness and was about to learn why: "The thing is, I'm here with a guy I'm kinda dating—and he's coming over right now."

"Oh shit, and I'm hitting on you," I said with a laugh. "No worries. Just tell him I'm your gay friend. Your GBF—your gay best friend. He'll be fine." She laughed and said okay.

The guy came over and looked at me with suspicion, wearing a forced smile. "Chad, this is Connell—my *gay friend*," Katie said. He relaxed. I was no threat, he thought. The three of us chatted, and I learned that Katie was a fitness influencer on Instagram.

I just needed to find a way to get her number. "Katie, I recently lost all my contacts," I said. "Can you give me your number again?" She shared her digits, and Chad was none the wiser.

I left the store and a few blocks later, my phone buzzed. "Very smooth. Nice meeting you, GBF. Maybe I can get you to switch teams ;) Katie."

Look, I'm not telling you to steal a guy's girl in front of him, but I'm not telling you *not* to. (If Katie were truly committed to him, she would have told me to buzz off, and she certainly wouldn't have texted me.)

At this point in your dating journey, you have all the pieces in place to enjoy a fulfilling love life. Still, it's good to have some advanced knowledge, because the search for your soul mate can throw surprises your way. Plus, it can be fun to show off.

Let's delve into some advanced dating situations, from approaching women while they're working (baristas, store clerks, etc.), to getting a girl's number when you barely have time to talk—in an elevator, say, or at a funeral home. (Kidding! Wait for the reception afterward.)

HOW TO GET HER
NUMBER IN SIXTY SECONDS

When you have little time to talk to a girl—you're late for work or sharing an elevator with an intriguing woman—you have to be direct but disarming. Suggest a sixty-second date. It goes like this: "Hi, I know this is random, but you're absolutely adorable. I have to go in a second, but how about we have a sixty-second date right now to see if we like each other? Up for it?"

It's a bold move yet a small ask—just one minute of her time. If she's single and likes your vibe, she'll likely say yes. After a minute (or two), get her number for your "second" date.

HOW TO MANAGE A MÉNAGE

According to a Kinsey Institute survey, 95 percent of men and 87 percent of women have fantasized about sex with multiple partners. But a separate study revealed that just 18 percent of men and 10 percent of women have actually had threesomes.[2]

The ménage à trois—it's one of those things that sound awesome but are hard to put together, like Super Bowl tickets or IKEA furniture.

The secret? You just have to ask the right way.

When I began casually dating Natalia, I decided to roll the three-sided dice. One afternoon, I sent her a carefully crafted text: "Hey, you! You can totally say no, but I was thinking . . . I've never been with two women, and I've always wanted to experience it with the right partner. I think it would be super sensual and amazing to do it with you. Thoughts? Maybe you have a girlfriend in mind? All good either way! Just wanted to ask."

I was nervous, but I hit "send." Then I waited and waited. No reply after several hours. I thought I must have offended her. Damn.

Not long after midnight, as I was nodding off, my apartment buzzer rang. It was Natalia, showing up unannounced with a bottle of wine and a female friend. It was a threesome-o-gram.

If you want to have a ménage à trois, bring it up early in the dating process—after the two of you have been intimate, but before you've defined the relationship. Frame it as a fun, sexy adventure to experience together. Make it an "us" thing, not a "me" thing. It's amazing what can happen when you ask nicely.

HOW TO INSTANTLY ESCAPE THE FRIEND ZONE

Okay, you're on a date, and you can feel yourself being too timid, quickly getting swallowed into the quicksand of the friend zone. What do you do? Make an ad hominem (Latin for "to the person") comment. In other words, a "you" statement. Say something positive and M-W about her ("You're adorable . . . ," "That look you gave me was R-rated . . . ," "You're so sexy when you XYZ . . ."). What you say is not that important, as long as it's something personal about her that sends an M-W impulse and snaps you out of your comfort zone.

HOW TO APPROACH A LARGE GROUP

If there are four or fewer women together in a bar or club, address the entire group as a unit: "Hey, you guys look stylish tonight." If there are five or more, approach the woman who most interests you and then have her introduce you to her friends.

HOW TO RECONNECT
WITH A GIRL WHO GOT AWAY

Here's what to text a woman whose number you got a few months prior, but you never followed up with, so the trail has gone cold. It's the Reconnect Text.

"I don't know, [name]. I feel like we're growing apart. It's like I don't even know who you are anymore. Have we lost that lovin' feeling? [[sad emoji]]"

She might not even remember you, but this playful salvo invites her to write back. A few messages later, you might have your long-overdue first date on your calendar.

HOW TO CHARM THE PERFECT 10

Every swan was once an ugly duckling, or at least felt like one. When you're talking to a woman whom most guys would consider a 10, ask her about her nerdy, dorky youth—and share a story or two from your nerdy high school days. This is not a tactic to make her feel insecure. On the contrary—thanks to you, she'll feel even sexier because you're contrasting her present-day beauty with the pimply, braces-wearing girl she used to be. It also creates a connection. When you're both being real and vulnerable, you'll stop seeing her as a number and start seeing her as a person.

HOW TO TURN YOUR INSTAGRAM
INTO A DATE GENERATOR

If you're a social guy with a cool lifestyle—into parties, clubbing, and travel—you can use your Instagram account to get dates. Bragging about those things in person kills attraction, but posting photos of the "good life" on your IG feed gets women's attention. It's the ultimate humblebrag. Simply post a few cool FOMO photos weekly. When you meet women, instead of swapping phone numbers, trade IG handles. They'll see your well-curated life and want to become a part of it.

HARNESS THE POWER
OF SOCIAL PROOF

When it comes to dating success, nothing is more important than being your most confident, authentic you. But there's a secret weapon that takes things to the next level: social proof, and its cousin, preselection.

Social proof[3] (a term coined by social scientist Robert Cialdini in his book *Influence*) is the phenomenon wherein people mirror the actions and beliefs of others. In dating, when a woman sees that other people like and approve of you, she's more apt to like you because she sees "proof" of your social value. (Social proof is evident everywhere, from Rotten Tomatoes rankings to Facebook likes to blurbs for this book.)

Preselection is similar to social proof, and is perhaps even more powerful. When a potential partner sees that you're "selected" by quality women, your perceived social value soars through the roof, and her romantic interest along with it. I was once in a Stockholm nightclub where I met a sexy artist named Astrid. She *kinda* liked me, but when she saw me with another stylish, beautiful Swede (who was just a friend), she reapproached me with much more interest, and we ended up spending the week together.

Social proof and preselection can propel you to greater heights. Here are two ways to put them to use.

FIND A WINGWOMAN

Better than any wingman is a sociable, stylish female friend to join you out on the town. A wingwoman has superpowers! All she has to do is socialize with you (in the presence of other women) and introduce you to girls and great things happen. Don't be shy about asking a friend or acquaintance if she wants the gig; women tend to love doing this. Make sure you offer her something in return, whether it's professional contacts, introducing her to cool, available men (if she's single), or just picking up her drinks tab for the night.

USE A ROMANTIC RECRUITER

Ask a sociable female friend to be your romantic recruiter, meaning she'll be on the lookout for good matches for you when she's out on the town. Yes, a wingman can do the same, but women trust other women in a way they don't trust men.

It works like this. Let's say your romantic recruiter meets a woman named Amanda, who's totally your type. Your pal can talk you up—"You seem like you might be good for my friend [your name]"—and then connect you both via text. Something like, "Amanda, meet [your name]! You two will hit it off." Now all you have to do is swap a couple friendly messages with Amanda and then ask her out. Your recruiter did the hard work, and you've got a hot date—and you didn't even have to leave your house!

CHAPTER 11 MISSION

Test-Drive One Advanced Ninja Move

Which of these techniques seems like the most fun for you to try? Go out and take it for a spin.

SO WHAT HAVE WE LEARNED?

....

- You don't need advanced moves to have a great dating life, but they can up the fun factor once you have the fundamentals down.
- Your authentic self is more important than any "move," but using social proof and preselection can take your dating results to a new level.
- Find a wingwoman. She'll be invaluable.
- Reason no. *trois* that you are enough: few things can boost your confidence like a ménage.

⚡ BONUS TIPS ⚡

DEVIOUS APPROACHING MOVES
....

These three semi-sneaky techniques can come in handy. Because (almost) all's fair when it comes to approaching.

PUT HER IN THE FRIEND ZONE
Turn the tables! Early in the conversation, tell her why you're *not* gonna have sex with her. "Oh, I can't hit the sheets with you tonight—I barely know you." This actually puts sex on her mind and sending her to the (pretend) friend zone can make a woman want to chase you.

CHARM THE "NOTTIE" TO ATTRACT THE HOTTIE
You'll sometimes find yourself talking to two women—one you're very attracted to, and one you're not. A simple rule? Flirt with the woman you like, and just be friendly with her girlfriend.

You can also flirt with the woman you like *through* her friend, turning her into a matchmaker, a role that women generally enjoy. "Stacey, tell me—is your friend Jenni here as cool as she seems, or should I head for the hills?" Don't think of the friend as the enemy. Make her your ally.

DO A "180"
With this move, you go from a warm, friendly opener to a negative spike that sparks attraction. You do a 180. The steps: 1) Compliment Her, 2) Ask Where's She's From, 3) Playfully Disapprove of Where She's From, 4) Just Chat, 5) Get Her Number. Here's how it ideally plays out, with a woman from California.

YOU: Excuse me, miss. Your leather boots are awesome. Great style.

HER: Hey, thanks!

YOU: [*surprised that she's so nice*] Wow, you're actually really friendly. Where are you from?

HER: I'm from California.

YOU: [*disapproving, but with a smile*] No! You're from Cali? I was afraid of that. That's too bad. Is it true what they say about women from California?

HER: [*more interested now, due to the emotional spike*] I don't know. What do they say?

YOU [share a stereotype]: You know, that you're all shallow, hippie, surfer chicks with plastic surgery. You seem nice, though.

HER: [*laughing and justifying herself*]: No, we're not all like that. I'm . . .

And then proceed as normal. This works because the friendly, indirect opener gets your foot in the door, and the strong negative spike gives her an emotional ride while she chases for approval.

The more conventionally attractive the woman is, the better it works, because they're not used to guys teasing them so casually and confidently.

CHAPTER 12

YOU FOUND THAT LOVIN' FEELIN'

> I love her and that's the beginning and end of everything.
> —F. Scott Fitzgerald, in a letter to Zelda Fitzgerald[1]

....

My client Richard (Higher Self name: "Slick Rick") had solved his biggest problem: not knowing how to talk to women. Now, he wanted more. He wanted a great girlfriend.

A real estate investor of Indian ancestry, Richard had only had one girlfriend by the time he reached his thirties. "In Indian families, you're encouraged not to date," he said. "You're taught to focus on studies and career and somehow you'll just magically get married. I never learned what women are like and how to flirt, and all these walls went up. I felt dysfunctional."

Working with me, Richard razed those walls and found himself dating a few women at the same time. But having a "roster" didn't fulfill him. He sought a relationship, preferably with Sarah, a kind, confident health-care worker he'd had a couple of great dates with. But he wasn't sure how to go about it.

"I was like, do you just ask? Or do I wait for her to bring it up? I wasn't sure."

I advised him to shift from Dating Mode to the Boyfriend Experience. That is, show the woman what a relationship with you would feel like. Basically, fake it till you make it . . . official.

Instead of going out for drinks and dinners, which they'd already done, Richard asked Sarah to pick out clothes with him at Urban Outfitters, attend yoga class together, and shop at Whole Foods. He introduced her to his friends and coworkers. He booked her for weekly dates. And soon she was reciprocating, asking him to join her and her girlfriends for brunch. "We both just clicked into these roles and it felt so natural," he said.

Richard asked Sarah to date exclusively, and she said yes. Eight months later, while vacationing together in San Francisco, he dropped to one knee and proposed—in the shadow of the Golden Gate Bridge, no less. Another yes!

When you've found The One—or at least, the one you want to be your girlfriend—it helps to have a plan. In this chapter, I'll give you the playbook to landing a great relationship. And I'll share the three questions to ask yourself to make sure that she's really the right woman for you.

SETTLE FOR MORE
....

When you enter a relationship, it will fall into one of four categories, depending on where you are in your search for love. Here they are, from worst to first.

Wrong Person, Wrong Time: This is when she's not a good fit for you, and you don't even want a relationship. But dating sucks, and you don't want to be alone, so you relent. The ultimate in settling.

Wrong Person, Right Time: You're ready to commit to *someone*, but you have a scarcity of options, so you settle for what you can get. This is most men, I believe.

Right Person, Wrong Time: You weren't looking for romance, but how could you not lock her down? She's awesome.

Right Person, Right Time: Brains, beauty, kind—the whole package.

She turns you into a human heart–eyed emoji, and you're ready to dive in. This is the ideal.

As men, deep down we all want true love, but we tend to settle for something comfortable and convenient. Something "good enough." But when you settle, you miss out on finding the right person.

Don't settle for "good enough." This is too important. It's your love life. Raise your standards and go after a truly great relationship with a quality woman who's right for you.

If you feel like she might be the right person at the right time, you need to ask yourself three important questions before pursuing a relationship with her.

1. **Do We "Just Fit"? Do your souls dovetail? Do you just fit? Listen to your gut.**

2. **Does Our Big Life Stuff Align? Are you compatible in areas such as core values, wanting a family, religious views, political beliefs, and cultural backgrounds? Granted, you may only want a girlfriend right now, not a wife, but a great relationship should have strong long-term potential. You may have stuff in common but to make it work long-term, you need most of your Big Life Stuff to align.**

3. **Will We Grow Together? Can you see the two of you growing together, complementing one another? Because if a relationship isn't growing, it's dying. There's no in-between.**

If you answered "no" to any of these questions, there's a chance you're not with the right person. You may be settling. Remember, you're a Radically Authentic guy with an abundance of dating options. Never settle.

If you answered "yes" to all three questions, then it's time to give her the Boyfriend Experience.

SEVEN WAYS TO
MAKE HER YOUR PARTNER
···

1. **Build Trust**

   Virtually all women want to trust their man. She likely won't become your girlfriend unless she can trust you. Communicate openly, be vulnerable, listen, be consistent in your actions, admit your mistakes, and always tell the truth.

2. **Bring Her Into Your Social Circle**

   I met my future girlfriend Diana in a bookstore's self-help section. Like many women of Asian heritage, she's beautiful, but her bravery and sense of adventure is what wowed me: She'd just moved halfway around the world to start a new career in the U.S.

   I wanted her to be my girlfriend, so for our second date, I invited her to sit in with my pub-trivia team, Trivia Newton-John. Why? Because pub trivia is awesome. (Fun fact: Blood donors in Sweden are sent a text when their blood is used.) Also, I wanted her to meet my nerdy friends and get a feel for what being my partner would be like. We were soon dating exclusively.

   Introduce your potential girlfriend to your pals, coworkers, or even members of your family. Don't have much of a social circle? Get on that! If you want to invite a woman into your awesome life, you must have an awesome life into which to invite her.

3. **Do Boyfriend/Girlfriend Stuff**

   After a few "regular" dates, have her, say, help you pick out new jeans, join you at the gym, or go grocery shopping (followed by you whipping her up a delicious dinner, of course). Bonus: This breaks up the predictable, let's-do-drinks model of dating and gives her some romantic variety.

4. **"Man Up" to Make Her Feel Safe**

    Women tend to want to date guys who make them feel safe. This makes sense. Evolution selected men to be protectors. Unlike your *Homo sapiens* ancestors, you don't need to spear a saber-tooth tiger to impress your partner. Just do some (nontoxic) manly stuff to give her that sense of safety. Such as . . .

    - Be fit. Women like muscles.
    - Catch the mouse or relocate the spider.
    - Start a campfire.
    - Change her tire.
    - Drive stick.
    - Be the one to lock the front door before bed.
    - Offer her your coat.
    - Place both hands on either side of her when she leans on a wall.
    - Assertively state date plans ("We're doing dinner Friday at eight at that Italian place you like.")
    - Carry her to the bedroom.
    - Oh, and fix stuff around the house. I'm no Bob Vila, but I once changed a date's light fixture and before I was off the stepladder she was dragging me into her bedroom.

5. **Show Her Your Generous Side**

    Be a good tipper—women notice that. And letting her know (in an unboastful way) about your charitable pursuits can be powerful, as Richard learned. "Volunteer work is important to me," he said. "I donate to fight animal cruelty, and I work with the Ronald McDonald House [to help sick children]. I'd mention this to women and they'd turn to putty. Women really do like nice guys."

6. **Schedule at Least One Date Weekly**
    The more often you see her, the more it feels like a real relationship.

7. **Pop the Question!**
    After dating this way for a month or two, it's time to make your coupledom official. Plan ahead. Make it a moment. Choose the right place and time to "pop the question"—say, during a relaxing day in the park, not in some loud bar.

    Be sincere. Speak from the heart. Tell her how much you enjoy her and what she's added to your life. (Should you use the L-word? Maybe! If you feel it, say it. If you don't, that can come later.) Say something like, "I'm crazy about you, and the way you [specific thing you love]. I don't want to date anyone else. I want to be your boyfriend. Would you like to be my girlfriend?"

    If she says yes, celebrate, laugh, kiss, and rip each other's clothes off. (If you're in a park, wait till you get home for that last part.)

    In the event she says no, it will sting. But listen. What are her reasons? Does she need more time? No matter what she says, be proud that you went for it.

THE PATH TO FULFILLMENT

When I struggled with women and started learning how to date, I thought that having a "rotation" would make me happy. It didn't—not for long, anyway. I'm cool with dating around for a while, but sex without love and true connection is just candy for the ego. There's a sugar rush but no real nourishment.

Dating to gratify your ego won't fulfill you because it's all about *you*. Romantic fulfillment comes from growing with, and giving to, a wonderful partner.

CHAPTER 12 MISSION

Give Her the Boyfriend Experience

If you're dating a woman you see as a possible girlfriend, put the concepts in this chapter into action.

SO WHAT HAVE WE LEARNED?

- Give her the Boyfriend Experience to help make the woman you're into your girlfriend.
- Do things like introduce her to your social circle, build trust, and find "manly" ways to make her feel safe.
- Playing the field can be fun, but dating multiple women will not lead to fulfillment long-term. Fulfillment will come when you make dating about growing and giving.
- What can I say? Chicks dig trivia nerds.
- As if you weren't already enough for wonderful women: You now know a fascinating fact about Swedish blood donors.

CONSENT IS SEXY

HOW TO DATE IN THE #METOO ERA

My liberation as a man is tied to your liberation as a woman.
—Tony Porter, author and activist, from his TED Talk[1]

....

Kiss her, I thought as we walked to the subway station. It's now or never.

When Stephanie and I stopped at a crosswalk near the end of our first date, I went for it. But she had been checking her phone, so when she looked up, my incoming lips must have seemed like a sneak attack. She recoiled, and I caught the corner of her pursed mouth.

"God, I'm so sorry," I said, feeling clumsy and creepy.

"Umm, it's okay," she said, vanishing down the steps to catch her train. "G'nite." There was no second date.

Looking back years later, I now realize my rookie mistake. I call it the Lunge.

It happens near the end of a date. Sensing that he's been playing it too safe, a guy feels the pressure to make a move to keep from getting friend-zoned. But he doesn't want his date to feel uncomfortable, especially in the

#MeToo era. Finally, feeling the need to do *something*, he goes for the kiss, like a quarterback heaving a desperation, fourth-down pass. Surprised, the woman either pulls back or endures an awkward lip-lock.

For many men, the #MeToo era has made dating seem more confusing than ever. As a good-hearted guy, you may feel caught between two extremes. On the one hand, you don't want to do anything inappropriate. Yet on the other, you may fear that doing nothing will lead to you hearing, "Let's just be friends."

New dating lines have been drawn, and you're not sure where they are. Can you approach during the day, or is that harassment? Should you ask for her number or give her yours? Do you need verbal consent before sex? Before foreplay? Before kissing? Before even touching her?

In this chapter, I'll address the biggest problems guys face while looking for love in the time of #MeToo. The great news? For men with integrity and good intentions, dating today is easier than you might think.

Also, I'll share a personal story about how a woman I know—a survivor of sexual assault—opened my eyes to the importance of #MeToo, and helped me become a better, more empathetic man.

IT'S #METOO, NOT #YOUTOO

As I tell my clients, the #MeToo movement affects men, but it's not *about* men. It's about awareness of the widespread mistreatment and abuse of women and girls; about empathizing with survivors and sufferers of that mistreatment; and about doing our part as men to make women's lives better. This cultural shift is welcome and long overdue.

Yes, men are understandably afraid of dating missteps, but that misses the point, which is empathy for women. Don't be that guy who because of #MeToo tells his date, "You'll have to make the first move now." Women hate that mentality because it shows a lack of understanding about the meaning of the movement. Plus, women still want men to be men. Understanding this will help you better connect with women.

JUST THE FAQS

Here are some of the most common questions men ask me about how to date in the #MeToo Era.

WHAT'S THE DIFFERENCE BETWEEN FLIRTING AND MISCONDUCT?

Flirting is showing romantic interest in a charming, light manner—and behaving appropriately based on how she responds. If she likes it, keep going. If she doesn't, wish her well and move on. You did not harass her by flirting with her. You simply took a shot at romance. There's nothing wrong with that.

In my view, misconduct or harassment is pursuing or imposing your sexual interest—often in a vulgar, deceptive, or manipulative manner—when a woman is clearly not interested. (But I'm not a lawyer, so I'm not giving you legal advice about what is, or is not, harassment in the eyes of the law.)

CAN I BE PERSISTENT WITHOUT BEING HARASSING?

Yes, if you're elegant about it. A simple rule: If she's obviously not into you, move on. If you're not sure if she's interested, try to find out in a respectful, charming way. The proper amount of persistence is sometimes rewarded. But persisting when there's no interest from her can become harassment.

For example, if you match with a woman on a dating app, and she doesn't reply to your first message in a day or two, she has not necessarily ghosted you; she may just be busy. Feel free to send a playful, positive follow-up message—say, a short P.S. to your opener ("By the way, I love your skydiving photo. How many jumps have you done?"). This approach will serve you well over time. Multiple women have told me, "I like your persistence."

If she doesn't reply after two or three messages, let it go. What you never want to do is get upset, negative, or judgmental. *That* can verge on harassment. Be like those finger-snapping Jets in *West Side Story*: "Keep coolly cool, boy." Most guys either give up too soon or overreact to an unreturned message. Find the sweet spot. Take a chance, persist with charm, and know when to move on.

IS IT OKAY TO DATE SOMEONE I WORK WITH?

I'm not a fan of office romances. Even if you and your crush are of equal status at the company, courting a woman you work with is courting disaster. A smarter strategy is to use the tools in this book to build an abundant dating life outside of work, keeping your office a romance-free space.

Absolutely DO NOT date or pursue a woman you supervise, manage, or have power over at work. It's just wrong, and it can lead to a hornet's nest of problems for you, her, and your company, such as harassment claims, accusations of unfair treatment by other employees, and litigation. Don't do it.

SHOULD I WAIT FOR A WOMAN I LIKE TO ASK ME OUT?

Hey, if she goes all Sadie Hawkins Day, be flattered, but don't wait for it. In general, you want to be the one moving things forward. About nine out of ten women prefer to be asked out rather than do the asking, according to *Psychology Today*.[2] Similarly, don't give her your number and leave it for her to contact you (unless she tells you she prefers this approach). You're the man. It's up to you to ask, and up to her to say yes or no.

CAN I STILL MAKE ROMANTIC GESTURES ON DATES?

Yes. Open doors, pick up checks, walk her to her car—while noticing how she's responding, of course. Just make sure to keep romantic gestures small. No lavish gifts, no flowers, no love poetry. You don't need to win her over. You're already enough. Oh! And definitely don't fly cross-country to surprise a woman you've never met in person with a box of Victoria's Secret lingerie. (See: "Desperate, Connell Being," Chapter 7.)

CAN I GO FOR THE FIRST KISS?

Yes. Just avoid the Lunge. Take stair steps to that first kiss, as I explain in Chapter 8. If you're on a date, greet her with a warm hug. Move on to playful taps on her arm or shoulder. Hold eye contact. Open up and connect emotionally. Notice if she's laughing, enjoying you, and initiating touch herself. Hold her hand. Is she holding yours back and leaning in? If yes, she's ready to kiss. Go. Now.

Save your lunges for the gym.

SHOULD I ASK FOR PERMISSION TO KISS HER?

Only if you're a time-traveling knight from Medieval Europe looking for love in the present day. (Hey, that's not a bad screenplay idea. Working title: *One Knight Stand*.)

I'm all about getting verbal consent for any sexual acts, as you're about to read. And asking a woman permission to kiss her may sound chivalrous. But it's just not sexy. A girl likes it when a guy can read her signals, build romantic tension, and then make the first kiss feel like it "just happened" at the perfect moment.

IS IT OKAY TO APPROACH IN THE DAYTIME?

Absolutely—when done with charm and a confident vibe. You might be surprised how well many women respond to this. I was at an outdoor mall one afternoon when I met Maggie. At the time, I was still battling approach anxiety. She could sense it, I think. After I got her number, she said, as if speaking to all single men, "You can come right up and talk to us. It's okay. We like it."

ANY TIPS FOR GETTING HER
IN THE MOOD WHEN SHE'S AT MY PLACE?

Buy a heart-shaped bed, and give the mirrors on your ceiling that Windex shine.

Sex may be on your mind, but don't make that the primary goal. Rather, help her feel comfortable. For the first fifteen or so minutes at your place, give her space. Don't try to kiss right away, even if you were hot and heavy back at the bar. Offer her a drink. Put on some music. Give her a tour. Do the "thing" you invited her over to do. (See Chapter 8.)

Once she's comfortable, pick up where you left off—again, *always* being aware of how she's feeling. If you start to kiss, you might be surprised. Some women will eagerly escalate on you because you helped them feel comfortable first.

IF SHE COMES OVER, SHOULD I EXPECT SEX?

Absolutely not. Getting intimate is possible, but don't expect it. And never pressure her for it. First, it's wrong. It's also highly ineffective. If she feels pressured, she may never want to see you again and might leave right then and there. When she comes over, a woman has many good reasons to not have sex, including:

- Fear of pregnancy
- Fear of assault
- Fear of STDs
- Not wanting to feel "slutty"
- Not knowing you well enough/not being comfortable enough with you yet
- Wanting to wait until you two are in a relationship
- Just because . . .

Every woman has her own rules for when she's ready for intimacy. Be 100 percent cool with that. Paradoxically, if you put zero-point-zero pressure on her, she will trust you more and grow comfortable, and getting physical may actually happen sooner than later.

SHOULD I GET VERBAL CONSENT FOR SEX? DOESN'T THAT RUIN THE MOOD?

Ruin the mood? What word is sexier than "yes" when said by the right woman?

Always get clear, enthusiastic verbal consent before engaging in sexual acts. A helpful tip: Ask in a sexy, turned-on way, rather than like an attorney deposing a witness. Think Barry White, not Barry Scheck. Here are some sexy ways to seek consent, act by act. (Some of these come from Amber Amour, a sex educator and the founder of Creating Consent Culture.)

- "Can I go down on you?"
- "Do you want me to keep going?"
- "How about we go into the bedroom and I [sexual act you want to do with her]?"
- "I want you. Should I put on a condom?"
- "Do you want to do it from the back?"
- "Do you like that?"
- "How about morning sex?"

If she says no at any point, stop immediately. As Amour writes in the *Huffington Post*, "There are many ways to accept your partner's 'no' including, 'okay,' 'no problem,' or 'I respect that.'" She astutely adds that "peacefully accepting rejection could potentially increase your chances of getting laid in the future!"[3]

Feel free to ask her to stay over. Some women need to sleep over and not have sex in order to feel safe enough to hook up the next time. When I began seeing Kristy, who would later become my girlfriend, we kept it PG-13 the first evening she came over. She spent the night, and the next morning she rolled over, woke me up, and things got all NC-17.

Far from being a mood killer, the more trust you build with her, the more you'll both enjoy intimacy whenever it happens—whether it's date two or date twelve.

WHAT IF WE'VE BEEN DRINKING? CAN WE STILL HAVE SEX?

Use your best judgment. Being buzzed is one thing, but a drunk woman cannot truly consent. Don't do anything sexual if she seems more than tipsy. This is to protect the woman as well as yourself.

WHEN WE HAVE SEX, HOW DO I PLAY IT THE MORNING AFTER?

Be sweet. Spoon and pillow-talk, if she likes that. Offer her breakfast and coffee. Either drive her home or order her a ride-share car.

Text her something sweet later in the day. Here are some messages to consider. Add all the heart-eye emojis that you want.

- "My bed smells like you. This is a good thing."
- "You were amazing last night, and you're making it VERY hard to concentrate on work."
- "This is my casual, chill way of saying that I had so much fun with you, and I'd love to see you again."
- "I can't stop thinking about you and the way you [fill in the blank]. Just wanted you to know."
- "I've never been SO glad to be SO tired. #TotallyWorthIt"

- "Two words: Mind. Blowing. Can't wait to see you
  again. How about [day you'd like to see her]?"

Hey, she hit the Egyptian cotton with you. It's your duty as a gentleman to help her feel great about her decision.

THE STORY OF ALEX

The deepest relationships can begin in the shallowest places.

Alex and I met at a nightclub in Las Vegas. She reminded me of a forties movie actress—blond, sardonic, and wickedly witty. Lauren Bacall could have played her.

We spent much of the weekend together. Alex wanted us to keep dating after Vegas. I didn't feel the same. I liked her, but I mainly saw her as a hookup—more proof that my dorky, dateless former self was gone. Gorgeous college coed? Check. And on to the next girl.

She was hurt, but we remained friendly. We mostly texted wisecracks to each other. (She loved ribbing me about our age difference, calling me "old man.")

Late one winter night, Alex sent me a panicked text. "Connell, something awful has happened! Just the worst thing that could ever happen."

I thought, *Did I get her pregnant?* I was a master at making it about me.

I called, and she sounded shattered. She told me that at a bar a couple of nights earlier, she had run into a man whom she knew. He roofied her drink, rendering her semiconscious, then took her to a hotel and raped her.

I was shocked. "I'm so sorry," I said. "I'm here for you whenever you need me."

In the months that followed, Alex and I spoke on the phone countless times. I did my best to comfort her through her panic attacks and thoughts about suicide. "I want to go to sleep and never wake up," she once said through tears. "I want to stop seeing that night."

Rape survivor Alice Sebold writes in her memoir *Lucky*, "I've always thought that under *rape* in the dictionary it should tell the truth. It is not just forcible intercourse; rape means to inhabit and destroy everything."[4]

Alex had opened a window for me into that destruction. I began to educate myself about violence against women. I had always known it was a problem. But I didn't know just how frequently women all over the world are murdered, raped, assaulted, sold, and vanished. It was astounding and appalling.

Not all of our talks were raw and intense. As time went on, Alex and I joked around a lot. She was there to comfort me when my mom died, and again a few weeks later when I was laid off from my magazine job. "They can't do that," she said. "That's discrimination against the elderly." I hadn't laughed so hard in a month. We had become close friends.

One night, I told her I was sorry for discarding her after our initial fling. She forgave me. What I didn't come out and say was that I felt ashamed for using her just for her body, because that's what her rapist had done.

During a Skype call one evening, Alex's blue eyes seemed especially sad. Therapy had been grueling that day, she said, because new memories from her assault had returned. "Awful things," she said.

Her distant tone scared me. "Hey, are you okay?" I asked.

"No," she said, her voice regaining some steel. "But I will be." She was so wounded and yet so strong. That's when I knew I was in love.

The next summer, we were both unattached. I told her I wanted to visit her. We spent most of three days together exploring her West Coast city. We seemed to fit so well together.

On the last night of my trip, we went to bed together for the first time since we'd met four years earlier. Cuddling only, no sex. I'd been with a lot of women. But just holding my best friend in my arms was the most romantic night of my life. (You know you're in love when a sleeping woman drools on you, and you find it adorable.)

We waited three months to become intimate. When it happened, we held hands a lot, and I took care not to brace her wrists, so that she would not feel restrained. I kept asking her, "Is it okay if I . . . ?" I always thought the phrase "making love" was just a cheesy euphemism for sex. I now understood the meaning. It means that every atom in you is focused on the other person feeling safe, loved, and desired.

Soon after, I told her I was in love with her. Because I'm a man and sometimes an idiot, the words came out during a moment of passion. Alex found this cliché to be hilarious. "Of *course* you say that while you're inside of me," she said with a laugh. She added, sweetly, "I'm not ready to say it back. But if you want to keep saying it to me, that would be okay." That melted me. I thought of a Paul Simon song, about how some people don't say "I love you" yet ache to hear the words said to them.

Our relationship ended abruptly over New Year's, near the anniversary of her assault. She couldn't be with anyone right now, she said. "I feel like I'm a piece-of-shit person, and I have to figure stuff out." I had suspected that living three thousand miles apart might be our main obstacle to making a relationship work. But that wasn't the only thing in our way. It's like there were three thousand more miles between the way she once saw herself and the way she saw herself now. How can you fall in love when you feel unlovable? Rape means to destroy everything . . .

I told her that she was a wonderful person, and that I would be her friend forever, both of which are true.

Two years after our breakup, we still text sometimes, and she seems to be in a good place. She said she was okay with my sharing this story. (She also called me a "dweeb" for being into musical theater.) I miss her a lot.

Alex awakened in me deep empathy for women, and helped me become far less self-involved. I wish it hadn't taken an unspeakable act of violence to open my eyes, but I'm still grateful for the clarity.

"I NEED YOU WITH ME"

What women want from men is authenticity. What they need is empathy.

When a man starts dating a woman, rejection is about the worst thing that can happen to him. What can happen to a woman is much worse. Eight out of ten have experienced sexual harassment.[5] About 20 percent of women are victims of date rape at some point in their lives.[6] And there's a one-in-four chance that the next single woman you meet was sexually abused as a child.[7]

The Greeks gave us the concept of eros, which is romantic/sexual love. They also gave us the concept of agape. This is a higher, selfless, unconditional love and compassion for all people. Besides enjoying eros with a given woman, a Radically Authentic man cultivates agape for *all* women, and for people in general.

"I need you with me," activist Tony Porter says in his TED Talk. Men need to know that "it's okay to promote equality. That it's okay to have women who are just friends . . . That it's okay to be whole."

I want you to feel confident in your worth, and to attract a wonderful woman into your life. It's why I wrote this book. But I also want you to know that the litmus test for being a man is not how good you are with women. It's how good you are *to* women.

CHAPTER 13 MISSIONS

Three Ways to Become a More Empathetic Dater

1. **Get Curious**

   Empathy is finding out how others feel and showing compassion for their feelings. Empathy has a close cousin: curiosity. Get curious about people. Strike up conversations with women and men, asking them about their lives and their feelings.

2. **Get Aware**

   As men, we're largely blind to the privileges we enjoy. We generally aren't sexually harassed or catcalled. For the most part, we don't have to fear sexual assault. When we're in a bad mood, no one blames it on our gender. You may never think about this. I know I didn't. There's no need to feel guilt or shame about that. Because now you know, and you can take steps to become more aware of privileges that we enjoy as men.

3. **Get Reading**

   The right book is a great way to open your mind to women's issues. Here are three titles to consider.

   - *Come as You Are*, by Emily Nagoski, PhD, the book your future partner wants you to read! This science-packed exploration of female sexuality is also damn funny. A section of one chapter is titled, "The Clit, the Whole Clit, and Nothing but the Clit." So help me God.

- *The Handmaid's Tale*, by Margaret Atwood, the iconic novel about what happens to society when women lose control over their bodies.
- *Wild*, by Cheryl Strayed, is more than a memoir about the author's 1,100-mile hike on the Pacific Crest Trail. It's also a gripping meditation on grief and a fearless look into the depth of emotions that a woman can experience when dealing with a traumatic event.

SO WHAT HAVE WE LEARNED?

- Beware of the Lunge! Instead, baby-step your way to the first kiss.
- #MeToo affects men, but it's not about men. It's about awareness of the widespread mistreatment and abuse of women and girls, as well as a call for men to express greater empathy for women.
- Yes, you can still "make moves." Women want you to. Just make sure you notice how she's feeling, and adjust your actions accordingly. A Radically Authentic man knows when to take a chance. He also knows when to back off.
- Women want authenticity and need empathy.
- Yet another reason to see your enough-ness: You're a compassionate, self-aware man who can see the world through women's eyes.

⚡ BONUS TIPS ⚡

WHY YOU SHOULD USE THE OTHER F-WORD

Do you think that men and women are equal, and should be treated equally?

Yes? Cool! Then you, sir, are a feminist.

If the word scares you, don't let it. All it refers to is the idea that men and women have the same social worth and should be treated as equals.

Also, men who are feminists are hot! Consider . . .

John Legend: *People*'s Sexiest Man Alive for 2019 has said that "all men should be feminists."[8]

Joseph Gordon-Levitt: His project HitRecord fights gender inequality, and online he has topped women's lists of MFILFs (Male Feminists I'd Like to Fuck).

Harry Styles: The singer supported the UN Women's campaign HeForShe.

Ashton Kutcher: He's an articulate crusader against human trafficking, a problem that overwhelmingly impacts women.

Jon Hamm: The *Mad Men* star advocates for educating men about gender-based violence.

Eddie Vedder: I can't understand a word he sings, but for three decades, Pearl Jam's front man has been loud and clear in his support for women's causes.

I'm not saying you need to trade your baseball cap for a pussyhat. Just understand that feminism is really about protecting women. What's manlier than that?

SEVEN DATING MISTAKES THAT WILL GET A GUY GHOSTED IN THE #METOO ERA

- Referring to his "crazy" ex with "all her drama."
- Saying, "But what did Louis C.K. do that was so wrong?"
- Not going down on her (if she wants him to), or not making sure she's sexually satisfied.
- Talking down to a waiter, server, or bartender.
- Telling a woman to smile.
- Calling a woman defensive or emotional.
- Talking over her/dominating the conversation.

THE SECRET TO TOTAL CONFIDENCE & ROMANTIC CONNECTION

The play's the thing.

—William Shakespeare, *Hamlet*

A great insight struck me on a night when I'd struck out.

I went solo to what is arguably New York's hottest club, a spot harder to get into than Harvard. It was packed with stunning women in tight, tiny dresses. I approached for a bit, and nothing really clicked.

But I didn't mind. I was in great spirits because it was my fortieth birthday. It was a night to pause and appreciate how much I had grown in the two years since I'd begun working on my dating life. Plus, I'd recently started seeing Carrie, a bright, beautiful graphic designer who I was starting to fall for. I felt hopeful and full of gratitude.

So I changed my plan. No pressure to approach. Instead, I would solely focus on enjoying this night. I would have fun on my own terms. As corny as it may sound, what's fun for me is giving. So instead of approaching women, I decided to simply share my good vibes with those around me.

I fist-bumped a well-dressed husband and wife ("I dig the threads, guys"). We got to talking about theater, and they turned me on to an improv community that would enhance my life for years to come. Next, I befriended a table of fun-loving Australian guys. One of them said, "Oi, mate! How do you talk to girls so easy?" So I gave him some tips. Then I saw a brunette, motioned for her to come to our table, and I introduced her to the Aussie. She was soon loving his accent, and I thought, *Man, this coaching stuff is fun.*

In short, I let go of chasing what I wanted and tried to give others what they wanted. It was my birthday, but I was the one handing out gifts. It felt so good.

After twenty years of hating dating, I finally loved it. And that very enjoyment of the journey, I realized, is what creates the "results" and romantic connections—not every day or night, perhaps, but definitely in the long term.

To get better at dating, find ways to *enjoy* dating. Fall in love with the process. Make it feel good. And share those good feelings with others. It's all about the feels.

You see, when dating feels bad, you take little or no action, your confidence sags, and your love life sucks. But when the process of dating feels good, you take tons of action, your confidence soars, and you start to attract the kinds of women you want.

This applies to so much in life. If something feels good, you'll do more of it and with your whole heart. Anything that you value and enjoy pursuing you tend to do more often, which helps you get better at it faster. Think of a rewarding hobby or passion—maybe it's traveling, working out, or playing a musical instrument. The reason you're so motivated by this thing is twofold: because it's *good* for you, and because it *feels* good. It's playtime, not work. That's what keeps you coming back.

Shakespeare wrote, "The play's the thing." Well, in dating, the thing's the *play*. A sense of fun and playfulness is irresistible to women. Have more fun and you'll get the girls. But more important, a playful approach will light *you* up and keep you taking action until you reach your Amazing Outcome.

Here's my vision for you. When you have fun with dating, you tip over a domino that starts a chain reaction. I call it the Upward Spiral of Abundance. It goes like this.

THE UPWARD SPIRAL OF ABUNDANCE
....

You start to take action, all excited about the outcome, and that feels good. Now you have momentum! This leads to *more* action and increased confidence. You start to numb yourself to blowouts and disappointments, realizing they can't hurt you, which leads to more action and more good mojo. And with all the reps you're getting—approaching, flirting, texting—your skills improve, and you meet more and more women. You get bolder. You take chances, doing great sometimes and fucking up other times. And it's all good! You're immersed in the journey.

And then it happens: You have a breakthrough. An experience blows your hair back, like the night I met Kelly, in Chapter 1. You make out with the beauty of the bar, or you have a date where you never run out of things to say, or you approach that Wow Girl and she likes you, or you launch a profile that fills your phone with matches . . . You'll know the breakthrough when it happens. And when it does, you'll have new proof of your worthiness, and you'll realize: *I'm enough. Women like me. I'm good.*

This epiphany unlocks a sense of abundance, both in the raw number of dating options you have and also an internal abundance. An endless stash of self-confidence. You realize that you're in any woman's league, and she'd be lucky to have you. This energy makes you even *more* attractive to women, because you have more to offer and zero neediness. And you're psyched to take *more* action, so the Upward Spiral continues. You ride this momentum until you meet a girl you deeply connect with, and you're able to choose a great partner from some wonderful options. ("I like Allison and Jennifer, but there's just something special about Erica. I think she's The One . . .") You get to settle *down*, not settle *for*.

That destination awaits you, but to reach it, you need fuel in the form of fun, playfulness, enjoyment. You need to love the process. (Or at least not hate it!) Find ways to enjoy dating on your terms, until you're attracting the kinds of women you've always wanted. Make dating a "feels good" experience.

- . . . . . It feels good to share honest, vulnerable truth with women.
- . . . . . It feels good to hang with your favorite wingman and meet girls together.

. . . . . It feels good to send silly Tinder openers that crack you up.

. . . . . It feels good to have pre-date butterflies.

. . . . . It feels good to accept yourself as you are right now—while still working on improving yourself.

. . . . . It feels good to be free from the fear of rejection.

. . . . . It feels good to grow as a man and give to a woman.

. . . . . It feels good to show your romantic intentions.

. . . . . It feels good to let go of approach anxiety.

. . . . . It feels good to look at dating as a way to play and have fun. (It feels good to women, too.)

. . . . . It feels good to hand the keys of your love life to your Higher Self, letting him see what this baby can do.

. . . . . It feels good to know that you're enough.

. . . . . And it feels good to strip away the doubt and fear and drill down to your core, revealing the diamond beneath: an authentic man of total confidence on his path to romantic connection and finding the perfect partner.

CHAPTER 14 MISSIONS
. . . .

Three Steps to Lock in Long-Term Success and Achieve Your Amazing Outcome

1. **Write Your "Feels Good" List**

   To take massive action in your love life and create that Upward Spiral of Abundance, dating needs to feel good. Cultivate enjoyment. Brainstorm ten things you can love about dating that are in your control. Focus on actions, rather than results. (Example: "It feels good to step up and ask out a woman I have a crush on.") Feel free to borrow ideas from this chapter but add your own, too.

2. **Create a Weekly Code of Conduct**

   A Code of Conduct is a commitment to the specific, measurable actions that you *will* take going forward to help you reach your Amazing Outcome. For example, you might write it like this: "Every week, I will go out for at least one hour to approach women, and I will spend at least two hours swiping on Tinder." Tip: Stretch your current comfort zone, but don't overdo it. If you've never approached a woman, don't commit to clubbing five nights a week. You'll burn out and get bummed out! One or two nights a week is plenty. Follow your Code of Conduct for one month and then reassess to make needed adjustments.

3. **Join My Facebook Group to Lock in Long-Term Results**
You now have everything you need to build confidence and attract a great girlfriend by being authentic. But if you want to lock in long-term success, join my Facebook Group, "How to Be Your Best Self—and Get the Girl." A secret to lasting results in any area is joining a community of people who share the same values and goals. In my private group, you'll be connected to thousands of cool guys all over the world. You'll be able to ask me questions, trouble-shoot sticking points, and celebrate your dating successes. Plus, I do live video training every month. Come and hang!
www.facebook.com/groups/howtobeyourbestself

SO WHAT HAVE WE LEARNED?

- Enjoying the process makes dating fun. If dating feels good, your Amazing Outcome is pretty much a done deal.
- Women love Australian accents. Ohio accents like mine, not so much.
- One final reason that you are enough: You finished this flippin' book!

⚡ BONUS TIP ⚡

SHOULD YOU DO IMPROV?
YES, AND . . .
....

Put down this book and sign up for an improv class. (Schools can be found in most major U.S. cities.) With its philosophy of saying "Yes, and . . ." to your scene partner, improv sharpens your wit, improves your listening skills, makes you better at connection, and massively enhances your playfulness—all qualities that take your love life to new heights. You'll also learn improv games that are fun to play on dates.

ADDITIONAL RESOURCES

Here are some of the best coaches, books, and podcasts I turned to while working on my dating life and my overall self-development. For an updated list of recommended books and podcasts, go to DatingTransformation.com and subscribe to my weekly column, "Ask the Dating Coach."

COACHES/SEMINARS

Tony Robbins
I've attended all the events that the iconic self-help coach headlines, and I think this is his neatest trick: Robbins is the one onstage, but he makes *you* feel like the rock star. (A heads-up: As of this writing, COVID-19 has forced his seminars online.) His "Date With Destiny" program is the best self-development event I've ever attended.

Jim Fannin
The funny, folksy, peak-performance coach has guided world-class athletes (Alex Rodriguez, Grant Hill), Fortune 500 CEOs (GE, Microsoft), and yours truly. He's about getting you out of your head and into "the zone" in almost any arena. I especially grooved to a concept he teaches called "the essence of the craft," wherein you distill a series of complex tasks into a single mantra, so you can perform under pressure (see Chapter 5). He shares tons of cool tools like that in his book *The Blueprint: A Proven Plan for Successful Living.*

Anthony Recenello
Before I hired Recenello, I had maybe taken one too many pickup programs and had become too "gamey"—that is, I would walk up to women and lean on button-pushing lines, rather than being present and real. I was often the

opposite of authentic. Recenello helped me smooth those edges. He imbues heart and class in an industry that can be sketch city.

Owen Cook

When I first sought out a coach to teach me the fundamentals of approaching women, I found a video in which Cook said, "Until you can walk up to any woman and be yourself, there's work to be done." That resonated with me, so I took multiple "in-field" boot camps with him in several cities. Equal parts thought leader and cult figure in the "pickup community," Cook, who now teaches self-development rather than dating advice, has been coaching men all over the world for well over a decade. (This is unknowable, but I wouldn't be surprised if he's approached more women than any man *ever*.) He was the first coach I found who taught dating success as a form of holistic self-development. On a more personal note, early in my journey, I was struggling with approaching, whining like a little baby, and was about to give up. Cook gave me a pep talk to make Knute Rockne proud and guided me to a huge breakthrough. I'll forever be grateful to him for that.

BOOKS

Think Like a Monk: Train Your Mind for Peace and Purpose Every Day by Jay Shetty

Whoa. A former Vedic monk, Shetty went to India and spent three years meditating up to *eight hours* daily. (I can't focus long enough to get through a *Peaky Blinders* episode.) The result is this empowering collection of wisdom. It brims with useful life advice that can also help your romantic fortunes, such as how to overcome negativity, how to get out of your head, and how to learn from everyone you meet. This pithy, practical gem about reframing a negative into a positive is my personal favorite: "Swap 'Why is this happening to me?' to 'What is this trying to teach me?' It will change everything." Shetty's hugely popular health and wellness podcast, *On Purpose*, is also worth checking out.

Daring Greatly: How the Courage to Be Vulnerable Transforms the Way We Live, Love, Parent, and Lead by Brené Brown

Ever since her 2010 TED Talk rightly garnered a gazillion views, Brown has become synonymous with the very word "vulnerability." Her elegant life-thesis is, You may think that being vulnerable is a sign of weakness, but it's actually a sign of strength. In my view, a man can't be fully authentic until he's embraced vulnerability.

Turning Pro: Tap Your Inner Power and Create Your Life's Work by Steven Pressfield

Warning: You may be living a "shadow" life, rather than the life of deep purpose you were meant to lead, Pressfield asserts. If you're willing to face that possibility, and do the hard work needed to set things right, this fast read is for you.

Can't Hurt Me: Master Your Mind and Defy the Odds by David Goggins

Goggins transformed himself from an obese exterminator and survivor of poverty and abuse into a Navy SEAL whom *Outside* magazine called one of the "fittest (real) athletes" in America. When I read this unflinching sentence, I dropped and did twenty push-ups: "You can be born in a fucking sewer and still be the baddest motherfucker on earth." Awe. Some.

Contagious: Why Things Catch On by Jonah Berger

A business book that can help your love life? Yes, if you use it that way. A marketing professor at Wharton, Berger shows readers how to make their products and ideas catch on using concepts that I feel can also be applied to online dating and texting. For example, he tells us that half of all tweets are "me"-focused, because sharing your own personal stories activates the same pleasure centers as money and food. This is why a Tinder message that asks a woman to share her weekend highlight or a viewpoint is more likely to get you a reply than a message that's all about you.

PODCASTS

U Up? with Jordana Abraham and Jared Freid

You will laugh. You will cringe. You will get solid advice when the witty hosts answer listener questions such as, "Is it possible to go from sexting to dating?" and "Why do people keep canceling on me before dates?"

The School of Greatness with Lewis Howes

The best-selling author of the book *The School of Greatness* helps listeners unlock their best selves with his podcast, welcoming the top achievers in areas like entertainment (Kevin Hart), sports (Dennis Rodman), and money management (Dave Ramsey).

Love Life with Matthew Hussey

Why listen to a podcast geared toward single women? Because Hussey is brilliant at articulating insights into how the opposite sex thinks. And the better you understand women, the better your dating outcomes will be. Speaking of understanding women . . .

Why Won't You Date Me? with Nicole Byer

"Why is Nicole still single?" Byer's own podcast description asks about the author and comedian. "She's smart, funny, has a fat ass, and loves giving blow jobs." That's the kind of raw, riotous truth-telling you'll get on this production. No matter the size of *your* ass, you'll laugh it off when you listen.

The Jordan Harbinger Show with Jordan Harbinger

Here are three reasons why this podcast is so damn good: 1) Harbinger has mastered the art of conversation, something to always be improving; 2) His diverse range of guests (Mark Cuban one episode, Bill Nye the next) offer practical life lessons; 3) The quirky stories covered give you handy, back-pocket talking points for your next date ("So this podcast had on a guy whose ex left him to become an escort . . .")

The Tim Ferriss Show with Tim Ferriss

The best-selling author of *The 4-Hour Workweek* talks with world-class performers (from athletes to investment experts to chess champions) and unpacks actionable advice that you can use. (A standout episode is called "How to Say No.")

The Art of Charm with Johnny Dzubak and AJ Harbinger

Two savvy hosts (and also dating experts) help you in arenas such as self-confidence, critical thinking, motivation, and career success—with lots of advice on women and dating, too.

The Art of Manliness with Brett McKay

With episodes titled "How to Develop Greater Self-Awareness" and "Life Lessons from Dead Philosophers," this program is tailor-made for the brainiac looking to improve himself. (My favorite: "How to Design Conversations That Matter.")

By the Book with Jolenta Greenberg and Kristen Meinzer

Congrats! You're done with *Dating Sucks, but You Don't*. But which self-help author should you read next? *By the Book*'s cohosts will help you decide. Each week they live by the rules of a different how-to title (say, *Getting Things Done* or *Who Moved My Cheese?*), and give it their thumbs-up or -down, with help from their husbands.

BUT WAIT, THERE'S MORE!

Do you like free stuff? So do I! (I never leave Denny's without pocketing a bunch of orange-marmalade packets.) For readers of this book only, I've created a portal on my website that's packed with additional advice. It includes advanced approaching strategies, screenshots of my Tinder text exchanges, funny dating-app openers, and an entire bonus chapter on the art of flirty conversation. Check it out.

www.datingtransformation.com/bonus

ACKNOWLEDGMENTS

Endless thanks to my agent Connor Eck and everyone at Lucinda Literary for taking my book idea from acorn to oak.

To my editor, Veronica Alvarado, who discovered me in a malt shop and said, "Kid, ya got something." (That's how I remember it, anyway.) Thank you for seeing value in my message, for your deft touch with a red pen, and for bringing me into the Tiller Press family.

A big, weepy bro hug to my buddy Nika Kartvelishvili, who did double duty as a line editor and a sounding board, helping me make my manuscript leaner and meaner. And thanks to Mark Beech and Dick "Fairway" Friedman for their astute editorial tweaks on select chapters.

A doffed cap and dropped jaw to Patrick Sullivan for his fantastic cover design, as well as to Jenny Chung for all her work in making the inside of the book look as good as the outside.

To my entire family, especially my dad, Denny Barrett, who taught me about integrity and hard work; and my niece, Delaney Sager, for letting me couch surf when I was first launching my biz.

A huge thanks to all of the dating coaches who mentored me, particularly Owen Cook and Anthony Recenello.

To every guy I've coached: thank you for placing your trust in me.

To the Fab Four who keep my company cranking: marketing wiz Aurelia Flores, web designer Laura Patricelli, videographer Juliet Clare Warren, and photographer/style expert/karaoke duet partner Riane Bawalan.

Thank you, Magnet Theater, for teaching me the life-changing magic of improv.

And to Kevin Cook, Jim Fannin, Matthew Harris, Amanda Bradford, Ally Fallon, Brooke Pullman, Cherlyn Chong, David Rein, Nick Kho, Dona Varghese, Keith Sabin, Brian Dunn, Chetan Narain, Bonnie Winston, Ione Butler, Jordan Carnduff, Angelique Hill Roebuck, and Jenni Cooper.

In the words of the T-shirt I'm wearing: "Fight evil. Read books."

NOTES

INTRODUCTION
....

1. Wilde, Oscar. *De Profundis*. 1900.
2. Liman, Doug. *Swingers*. 1996.
3. Nin, Anaïs. *Seduction of the Minotaur*. 2012.
4. Strauss, Neil. *The Game: Penetrating the Secret Society of Pickup Artists*. 2005.
5. Kafka, Franz, in a letter to Oskar Pollak. 1903.
6. Epictetus. *Enchiridion*. 2020.

CHAPTER 1: KEEPING IT REALLY REAL:
RADICAL AUTHENTICITY
....

1. Gervais, Ricky. Twitter post. March 1, 2019, 5:42 p.m. https://twitter.com/rickygervais/status /1101613814376738816?lang=en
2. Ravenscraft, Eric. "Practical Ways to Improve Your Confidence (and Why You Should)." *New York Times*. June 3, 2019.
3. Brown, Brené. *The Gifts of Imperfection: Let Go of Who You Think You're Supposed to Be and Embrace Who You Are*. 2010.
4. Josephs, Lawrence, et al. "Be yourself: Authenticity as a long-term mating strategy." *Personality and Individual Differences* 143, June 2019: 118.
5. Vonk, Roos. "The slime efffect: Suspicion and dislike of likeable behavior toward superiors." *Journal of Personality and Social Psychology* 74 (4), 1998: 849.
6. Shea, Amanda, and Jen Bell. "We asked 64,000 women what they look for in a partner. The most important thing? Kindness." Helloclue.com. November 10, 2019. https://helloclue .com/articles/sex/idealpartner

CHAPTER 2: "YOUR LOOKS MATTER"
& OTHER DATING MYTHS
....

1. Rifkin, Glenn. "William Goldman, Screenwriting Star and Hollywood Skeptic, Dies at 87." *New York Times*, November 16, 2018.
2. Davis, Allison P. "What Makes an Ideal Guy in 2016." *Glamour*. January 13, 2016.
3. Howes, Lewis. *The Mask of Masculinity: How Men Can Embrace Vulnerability, Create Strong Relationships, and Live their Fullest Lives*. 2017.
4. TruTV. "Adam Ruins Everything—Alpha Males Do Not Exist." YouTube video, 4:40. August 4, 2017. https://www.youtube.com/watch?v=OTi86veZBjU

CHAPTER 3: YOUR SUCKY LOVE LIFE IS YOUR FAULT (AND THAT'S A GOOD THING): BUILDING CORE CONFIDENCE

1. Proust, Marcel. *Swann's Way: In Search of Lost Time,* Volume 1. 2004.
2. White, Jules. *Calling All Curs.* 1939.
3. Robbins, Tony. *Unlimited Power.* 1986.
4. Clear, James. *Atomic Habits: An Easy & Proven Way to Build Good Habits & Break Bad Ones.* 2018.
5. Mills, Jarrod. "Tips for Making Sure Your New Year's Resolutions Stick." *Times-Tribune,* January 3, 2020.

CHAPTER 4: FOR ADDED VALUE, ADD SOME VALUES

1. Sun Tzu. *The Art of War.* 2010.
2. Pressfield, Steven. *The War of Art: Break Through the Blocks and Win Your Inner Creative Battles.* 2013.
3. Robbins, Tony. *Awaken the Giant Within: How to Take Immediate Control of Your Mental, Emotional, Physical & Financial Destiny!* 2007.

CHAPTER 5: HOW TO IGNITE ROMANTIC CONNECTION

1. Lawrence, D. H. *Studies in Classic American Literature.* 1923.
2. Shaywitz, B., S. Shaywitz, K. Pugh, et al. "Sex differences in the functional organization of the brain for language." *Nature,* February 1995: 607.

CHAPTER 6: ARE YOU MANLY ENOUGH TO BE FEMININE?

1. Hemingway, Ernest. "A Man's Credo." *Playboy,* January 1963.
2. Marche, Stephen. "Down in Havana, Searching for the Ghost of Hemingway." *Esquire.* October 1, 2015.
3. Human Activity System 2. "Charles Bukowski Kicking His Woman & Shit." YouTube video, 1:02. July 31, 2013.
4. Jung, Carl. *The Red Book: Liber Novus.* 2009.
5. Welch, Will. "Introducing GQ's New Masculinity Issue, Starring Pharrell," *GQ,* October 15, 2019.
6. Burriss, Robert P. "Why Certain Women Prefer a Man Who's More Feminine." *Psychology Today.* December 6, 2017.
7. Turner, Page. "Why I Only Date Men Who Are in Touch with Their Feminine Side." Bolde.com. 2017. https://www.bolde.com/date-men-touch-feminine-side/
8. Kim, John. *I Used to Be a Miserable F*ck: An Everyman's Guide to a Meaningful Life.* 2019.
9. Howes. *The Mask of Masculinity.*
10. Porter, Tony. "A Call to Men," filmed December 2010 in Washington, D.C. TED video, 10:58, https://www.ted.com/talks/tony_porter_a_call_to_men?language=en#t-10618

CHAPTER 7: IT'S NOT YOU—IT'S THE HALIBUT YOU'RE HOLDING: HOW TO GET GOOD AT ONLINE DATING

1. Palahniuk, Chuck. *Fight Club*. 2005.
2. Hakala, Katie. "This Is Why Men Outnumber Women Two-to-One on Tinder." February 18, 205. https://www.mic.com/articles/110774/two-thirds-of-tinder-users-are-men-here-s -why
3. "Online dating trends: Men outnumber women on Tinder by 9 to 1 (while Grinder wins for age diversity)." Netimperative.com. April 5, 2019. http://www.netimperative.com/2019/04/05 /online-dating-trends-men-outnumber-women-on-tinder-by-9-to-1-while-grinder-wins -for-age-diversity/
4. "Modern Dating Myths," Tinder. April, 2017.
5. Anderson, M., E. Vogels, and E. Turner, "The Virtues and Downsides of Online Dating." Pew Research Center. February 6, 2020.
6. Iqbal, Mansoor. "Tinder Revenue and Usage Statistics." Businessofapps.com. June 23, 2020. https://www.businessofapps.com/data/tinder-statistics/
7. Kercher, Sophia. "First Comes Tinder. Then Comes Marriage?" *New York Times*. April 19, 2017. https://www.nytimes.com/2017/04/19/style/tinder-relationship-dating-study.html
8. *Mad Men*. "Smoke Gets in Your Eyes." Directed and written by Matthew Weiner. AMC, July 19, 2007.
9. Zickl, Danielle. "This One Easy Dating Profile Tweak Could Get You Way More Matches." *Men's Health*. November 27, 2017.
10. *Seinfeld*. "The Opposite." Directed by Tom Cherones, and written by Larry David, Jerry Seinfeld, and Andy Cowan. May 1994.

CHAPTER 8: YOU HAD ME AT HELLO: GREAT FIRST DATES

1. Williams, Tennessee. *A Streetcar Named Desire*. 2004.
2. "Romantic-Comedy Behavior Gets Real-Life Man Arrested." *The Onion*. April 7, 1999. http://local.theonion.com/romantic-comedy-behavior-gets-real-life-man-arrested -1819565117
3. Huang, Karen, et al. "It Doesn't Hurt to Ask: Question-Asking Increases Liking." *Journal of Personality and Social Psychology*. Vol. 113, No. 3: 430.
4. https://www.menshealth.com.au/study-clothes-make-people-more-competent
5. Corsillo, Liza. "This Is the Underwear That Women Want You to Wear." *GQ*. September 23, 2016. https://www.gq.com/story/underwear-women-want-you-to-wear
6. *Esquire*. "What Women Want their Men to Wear," February 28, 2006.

CHAPTER 9: GET YOUR HEAD OUT OF YOUR APPS: HOW TO APPROACH AND CONNECT (PART 1)

1. Namath, Joe. Brainyquote.com.
2. Winch, Guy. "10 Surprising Facts About Rejection," *Psychology Today*. July 3, 2013. https:// www.psychologytoday.com/us/blog/the-squeaky-wheel/201307/10-surprising-facts-about -rejection

CHAPTER 11: ADVANCED NINJA MOVES
....

1. Needham, Hal. *Smokey and the Bandit.* 1977.
2. Hunt, Elle. "The Psychology of the Threesome: Everyone Wants One, but Who's Truly Ready for It?" *The Guardian*, February 11, 2020.
3. Cialdini, Robert. *Influence: The Psychology of Persuasion.* 2006.

CHAPTER 12: YOU FOUND THAT LOVIN' FEELIN'
....

1. Fitzgerald, F. Scott, and Zelda Fitzgerald. *Dear Scott, Dearest Zelda: The Love Letters of F. Scott and Zelda Fitzgerald.* 1985.

CHAPTER 13: CONSENT IS SEXY: HOW
TO DATE IN THE #METOO ERA
....

1. Porter. "A Call to Men."
2. Mills, Michael. "Why Don't Women Ask Men Out on First Dates?" *Psychology Today.* April 30, 2011.
3. Amour, Amber. "35 Sexy Ways to Ask for Consent." *Huffington Post.* April 28, 2017. https://www.huffingtonpost.co.uk/amber-amour/35-sexy-ways-to-ask-for-consent_b_9789458.html
4. Sebold, Alice. *Lucky.* 2009.
5. Chatterjee, Rhitu. "A New Survey Finds 81 Percent of Women Have Experienced Sexual Harassment." NPR.org. February 21, 2018. https://www.npr.org/sections/thetwo-way/2018/02/21/587671849/a-new-survey-finds-eighty-percent-of-women-have-experienced-sexual-harassment
6. P, Kim. "Date Rape Statistics." CreditDonkey.com. August 22, 2018. https://www.creditdonkey.com/date-rape-statistics.html
7. Centers for Disease Control. "Sexual Violence Is Preventable." CDC.gov. https://www.cdc.gov/injury/features/sexual-violence/index.html
8. Vincent, Alice. "John Legend: 'All Men Should Be Feminists.'" *The Telegraph.* March 27, 2013. https://www.telegraph.co.uk/culture/music/rockandpopmusic/9956410/John-Legend-All-men-should-be-feminists.html

ABOUT THE AUTHOR

The founder of Dating Transformation and a dating coach for The League, Connell Barrett helps men gain confidence and date wonderful women by embracing authenticity. He has helped men all over the world find love, from New Delhi to New York, where he lives. Connell is an advisor for AskMen and Elite Daily, and has appeared on *Access Hollywood* and *The Today Show*, as well as in *Playboy*; *Cosmopolitan*; and *O, The Oprah Magazine*. When he's not coaching men or performing musical improv, he's playing pub trivia with his team, Trivia Newton-John. You can read his weekly advice column, "Ask the Dating Coach," at DatingTransformation.com.